EXQUISITE
EXQUISITE
E

SP
SendPoints

REMARKABLE GRAPHIC STYLES EXQUISITE

Second printing of the first edition, January 2020

EDITED & PUBLISHED BY SendPoints Publishing Co., Ltd.

PUBLISHER: Lin Gengli

PUBLISHING DIRECTOR: Lin Shijian

ASSISTANT PUBLISHING-DIRECTOR: Chen Ting

CHIEF EDITOR: Lin Shijian

LEAD EDITOR: Li Weiji

EXECUTIVE EDITOR: Peggy Deng

DESIGN DIRECTOR: Lin Shijian

EXECUTIVE ART EDITOR: Kit Leung

PROOFREADING: James N. Powell, Peggy Deng

REGISTERED ADDRESS: Room 15A Block 9 Tsui Chuk Garden, Wong Tai Sin, Kowloon, Hong Kong

TEL: +852-35832323 / **FAX:** +852-35832448

OFFICE ADDRESS: 7F, No.9-1 Anning Street, Jinshazhou Road, Baiyun District, Guangzhou, China

TEL: +86-20-89095121 / **FAX:** +86-20-89095206

BEIJING OFFICE: Flat 1701, Block C, BBMG International, Wangjing West Road no.48, Chaoyang District, Beijing, China

TEL: +86-10-84139071 / **FAX:** +86-10-84139071

SHANGHAI OFFICE: Room 302, Floor 3, Ningbo Road no.349, Huangpu District, Shanghai, China

TEL: +86-21-63523469 / **FAX:** +86-21-63523469

SALES TEAM

UK, Europe, Africa, Oceania: Sunnie sales02@sendpoints.cn

America, the Middle East: Mia sales03@sendpoints.cn

Asia: Hedy sales01@sendpoints.cn

TEL: +86-20-81007895

EMAIL: sales@sendpoints.cn

WEBSITE: www.sendpoints.cn / www.spbooks.cn

ISBN 978-988-78494-7-6

Printed and bound in China.

CONTENT

EXQUISITE HERITAGE

Chinese embroidery, Kyō-Satsuma ware, Gong-bi painting, Indian pattachitra, Islamic mosques, Azulejo, stained glass in churches and palaces, Byzantine mosaics, Persian carpets, illuminated manuscripts... This list could go on and on. For each of these enchanting art genres of profound aesthetic value, which word would you use to describe it: "breathtaking," "splendid," "impressive," "captivating," "fascinating," "specular," or, "miraculous"?

Compared to these remarkable artworks, any such words might pale. Yet wherever words might fail, our hearts would throb and thrill. These stunningly beautiful and exquisite creations remain as emblems of our best artistic endeavors. The resources poured into them in various times and regions testify to artists' endless quests for a higher aesthetic. Most of all, they offer glimpses of the greatness of the civilizations that produced them.

In this book, we hope to follow our predecessors' footprints in pursuing exquisite beauty. We seek also to explore the possibilities of how this style might blaze new trails in contemporary graphic design world.

Stained glass windows in the Cathédrale of Saints-Michel-et-Gudule in Brussels

Chinese Embroidery

Embroidery has evolved over the last 3,000 years of Chinese history. The spectacular variety of geographical and ethnic features thriving in the vast land of China catalyzed a rich portfolio of embroidery schools: each with its distinct identity. The many needling techniques and stitches testify to a rich artistry, to intricate detail, to captivating finishes, and to rich symbolic denotation. Embroiderers would spend weeks, months, and even years on each piece, attentively and cautiously applying each movement of needlework on satin, silk, chiffon, or other fabrics after thorough planning and ingenious incorporations of engraving, calligraphy, and painting into the embroidery. Fine silk as thin as hair, which could be split into 96 finer strands by the hands of a master, would be categorized according to its subtly varied thickness and then be combined to produce patterns that deliver immaculate presentations from every angle.

The ubiquitous symbolic references in traditional Chinese embroidery are achieved through various rhetorical devices such as simile, homophony, and metonymy: with dragons symbolizing nobility and power, red bats signifying great blessings, and pomegranates denoting fertility. Whether it be magnificent dragon robes for emperors or embroidered bedcovers for common households, exquisite Chinese embroidery is a living expression of sincere wishes for a better life: for aesthetic refinement in the essence of a culture cherished and passed down from ancestor to ancestor.

Image/

Rank badge with qilin from late Qing dynasty

A rank badge was a square embroidered textile sewn onto the court robes of officials to signify the rank of the official. This rank badge with qilin indicates that the official once wearing it was a military official of the first rank.

Legend has it that there is a vase containing sticks placed in a pavilion in an immortal land. The sticks symbolize longevity and whenever cranes add sticks in the vase, one's life can be extended. This is an auspicious pattern common in uses for birthday celebration.

Silk embroidery on satin with cranes
over the immortal land from Qing Dynasty
Qianlong period

Embroidered Textile of the
Bodhisattva of Transcendent Wisdom
Qing dynasty

Illuminated Manuscript

With an origin that can be traced back to antiquity, illuminated manuscripts are handwritten books distinguished by a surprising detail of rich ornamentation, including gold or silver; elaborate miniatures; decorative margins and borders; and historiated initials and carpet pages. As rare and costly commodities, most of these books served as religious, devotional testaments or as status symbols commissioned by the powerful and the rich.

They were transcribed and illuminated by scribes and illuminators who supplied the text, the figurative paintings, and the pictorial embellishments. With valuable resources, which could be precious stones or vellum, and toilsome manual efforts, which could well be translated into years of labor for one book—these exquisite scripts are emblems of sincere dedication. They are important references for our study of calligraphy, painting, and bookbinding as well as the enduring aesthetic values that travel across time and space.

Image /

These two pages are from a Book of Hours which can be dated back to about 16th century. The text was made then and the illustrations were finished in about 19th century. The size of this manuscript is 12 cm wide and 17.5 cm high.

Missa quinqz plagarum :- S.

HVMILIAVIT
semetipsuz
dominus ie
sus xps us
qz ad morte.
mortem au
tem autem crucis: propter qd
deus exaltavit illum: et dona
vit illi nomen quod est super
omne nomen: Vs: Misericor
dias domine in eternum can
tabo in generatione et progenie:
Gloria patri:
Kyrieleison.
Kyrieleison.
Kyrieleison.
Xpisteleison

Incipiunt septem gaudia beate marie
Virgo templum trinita
tis. deus summe boni
tatis. et misericordie.
Qui tue humilitatis
dulcorem suauitatis
vidit et flagrancie. de te nasci nunciatur

Page from a manuscript of ca. 1460

This is the front cover of a richly decorated manuscript which dates back to the 17th century. It was a patent of nobility given by a Spanish King to a nobleman.

Persian Carpet

One of the most intriguing attributes of Persian carpets lies in their vast varieties of distinctive patterns: because each piece is one of a kind. There are meandering vines and tendrils, thriving trees, flowers in clusters, lively animals, and geometrical patterns interweaving rectilinear or curvilinear combinations as well as ample pictorial narratives, many tightly interwoven in richly elaborated and sophisticated overall designs.

Passed down from at least 2,500 years ago, this type of carpet weaving represents one of the most time-consuming and labor-intensive handicrafts in the world. Because it is based on techniques of tying knots—which can amount to as many as millions in a one-square-meter textile—the carpet produced will be incomparably tight and durable. From shearing fine and long-fibered wool, to dyeing using natural substances, to composing a detailed " cartoon " (sketch), to stringing, and knotting threads one by one, a piece of Persian carpet could take months, or even years. Inheriting great historical and cultural value, Persian carpets are cherished household decorative items that bear witness to people's lives for one generation after another.

Image /

This Schwarzenberg Carpet is from 16th century Iran. Animals and plants are depicted in this textile. Its size is 517 cm long and 217 cm wide.

Carpet with flying cranes and beasts,
probably produced in 16th to 17th century in Kashan, Iran

Pattachitra

In Eastern India lies Raghurajpur, India's first heritage crafts village: well known for its splendid pattachitra art. Pattachitra—formed from the Sanskrit words patta, meaning "cloth" and chitra, meaning "paintings"—refers to a traditional type of painting on cloth that exhibits a fascinating and vigorous play of sharp colors, delicate pictorial constructions, and exuberant decorations representing myths, religious stories, and folklore. Originating in the 5th BC, the art of pattachitra has been practiced and carried on by generations of traditional painters called Chitrakars, who always base their painting studios at home. Behind the captivating canvas, the sophistication and arduous efforts put into pattachitra lie far beyond what the eyes can capture. Besides making natural paints extracted from plants and minerals, the preparation phase of pattachitra requires a lengthy process of washing, coating, pasting, drying, and polishing the cloth before precisely applying lines. The outcome is a bright chromatic performance of primarily red, yellow, and indigo blue that pulsates with vividly and exquisitely delineated narratives wherein one can sense idiosyncratic and merry visions of Indian life.

Image /

Indian Patta Painting
©Ben30ghosh /
Wikimedia Commons / CC BY-SA 4.0

Indian Cloth Painting

Byzantine Mosaic

Solemnly peering down at pilgrims and visitors for centuries reign the magnificent mosaic wall paintings in Hagia Sophia, Basilica San Marco, and Basilica of San Vitale. This kind of mosaic painting: marked by glamorous and dominant gold backgrounds, glistening surfaces, and bright color palettes, reached a zenith of perfection during the reign of the Byzantine Empire (or called Eastern Roman Empire). Though later migration and appropriation took place in different regions, the genre is by and large referred to as "Byzantine mosaic." This distinctive pictorial decoration for eulogizing holy figures and royal families in churches was put together using thousands of colored-glass cubes, or tesserae in Latin, besides mother of pearl and gold or silver leaf. These glossy cubes were not only cut into varied sizes for different components, but also set at oblique angles to embrace and refract light penetrating inside through windows, bringing out a sparkling and otherworldly ambience reminiscent of a heavenly realm. Underneath the shimmering surface of the mosaic paintings often lies a detailed preliminary sketch that directs the overall decorative scheme. More important, however, is the accumulated knowledge and the refined craftsmanship.

Image/

Mosaic painting describing bible story

Mosaic of the Virgin Mother with child in north dome of narthex from the Church of the Holy Saviour in Chora, Istanbul

GEHON
CIVITAS DEI

Mosaic ceiling at the entrance
of the Cathedral of Aachen
Photo by Jebulon

Baroque Art

The term "Baroque" is derived from Portuguese barocco, meaning "imperfect pearl." This stylistic designation, denoting an irregularity and deviation from the classical and usual formal orders, refers to a grandeur artistic style that spanned from the 17th to the 18th century. Initially serving the needs of the Catholic Church to reaffirm its supreme authority, Baroque art assumed a propagandist role to impress visitors with a projection of power, majesty, and glory. Ignited in Italy, the Baroque craze soon spread and migrated to most parts of Europe, giving rise to manifold mutations of this passionate and elaborate artistic vision.

Featuring exuberant detail, captivating theatricality, dramatic lines, and dynamic movement, it incorporated various media—painting, architecture, dance, literature, theatre, and music—to arrive at a unified effect. From the tenebroso painting by Caravaggio, spotlighting the subject against darkness to emphasize a dramatic effect, to the illusionistic ceiling frescoes by Pietro da Cortona, to the breathtaking St. Peter's Baldachin by Bernini, to the flamboyant and lavish laces and ribbons ornamenting bourgeoisie and upper class's clothing, baroque art dazzled and sparkled, attesting to humanity's departure from the Renaissance and entrance into a flourishing of a significant style in the realm of Western art.

Image /

Inner view of the Church of
San Antonio de los Alemanes in Madrid
© Pier Paolo Cedaro, Flickr / CC BY-ND 2.0

Baroque ceiling frescoes

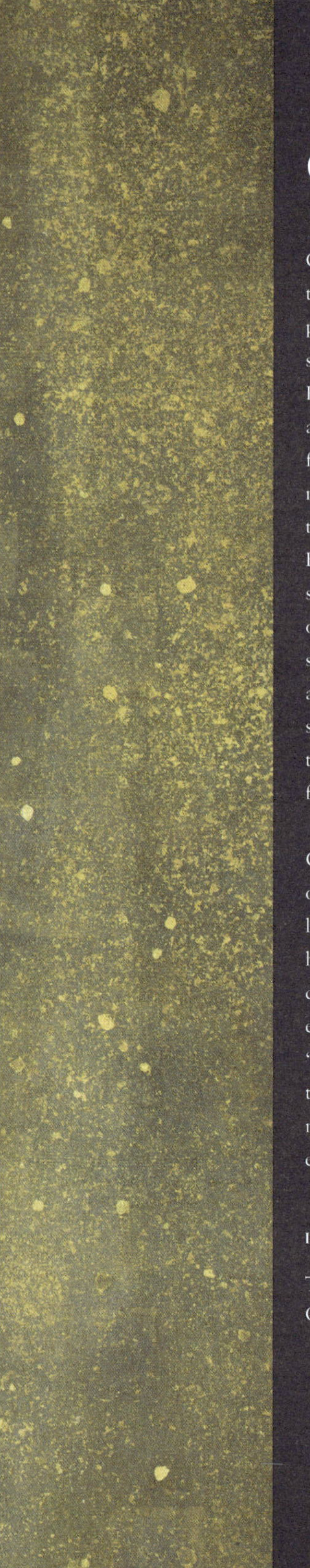

Gustav Klimt

Gustav Klimt (1862 – 1918), one of the founders of the Vienna Secession Movement, was an Austrian painter well noted for his bold rendering of intensive decoration and enchanting female portraits. In Klimt's unique combination of symbolic patterns, asymmetrical compositions, and mosaic-like finishes, one might find the influences of the Japanese Rinpa School, Byzantine imagery, and Egyptian motifs. His famous painting Portrait of Adele Bloch-Bauer sparkles with the luster of gold and silver paints, along with a kaleidoscopic gathering of vivid colors in emphatic whorls and coils. The subject, Lady Adele, is elegantly portrayed with a graceful, voluptuous body lines and an inaccessible, ineffable expression: just as mysterious as that featuring his other daring representations of female images.

Contrary to his excessive indulgence in sumptuous ornamentation and figurative patterning, Klimt led a reclusive and simple life. He devoted most of his time to his paintings, most of which epitomized deliberate and arduous efforts by the painter and even his subjects. The painter saw himself as only "a painter who paints day after day from morning to night," yet his paintings shimmer and glisten, never ceasing to startle and mesmerize viewers even till this day.

Image/

The Kiss
Oil on canvas created by Gustav Klimt

Portrait of Adele Bloch-Bauer I
Gustav Klimt

The Embrace
Gustav Klimt

William Morris

Among the many figures standing up against the overwhelming torrents of industrial expansion, William Morris (1834 – 1896) is one who confronted it with beautiful and delicate designs, showing how fine art can be united with decorative art. Born in Victorian Britain, Morris created plenty of elaborate and exquisite patterns for textile and wallpaper, besides being a prolific and versatile contributor to the era as designer, craftsman, poet, and socialist activist. His fascination with medievalism as well as his curiosity about Islamic, Indian, and Western sources led him to incorporate emblematic motifs and classical manners into his designs, offering intricacy and elaboration that pivots on mesmerizing repetition and symmetry. A fervent advocator of beauty as "a positive necessity of life," he learned and mastered various crafts in his lifetime—including embroidery, printing and dyeing. In addition, he even revived several lost techniques, unceasingly aspiring for higher excellence.

His beautiful and stylized floral patterns and hand-processed textiles, compared to chintzy machine-made products, became a source of nourishment for finer tastes and a continuous inspiration.

Image/

Jasmine
Wallpaper designed by William Morris

RUBÁIYÁT OF OMAR KHAYÁM

Sometimes I think that never blows so red
The rose as where some buried Cæsar bled
That every hyacinth the garden wears
Dropped in its lap from some once lovely head

XIX

And this delightful herb, whose tender green
Fledges the river's lip on which we lean —
Ah, lean upon it lightly! for who knows
From what once lovely lip it springs unseen!

XX

Ah, my Beloved, fill the cup that clears
To-day of past regrets, and future fears!
Tomorrow? Why, tomorrow I may be
Myself with Yesterday's seven thousand years

A page from an illuminated manuscript of the Rubaiyat of Omar Khayyam, an 11th century Persian Poet.
Calligraphy and ornamentation by William Morris, illustrations by Edward Burne-Jones

Willow Bough
Wallpapers designed by William Morris

Daisy

Wallpapers designed by William Morris

EST
LIMITED
Black
BY ORIGINAL
1920
SUPERIOR
CRAFT

Superb Craftsmanship

Superb craftsmanship or technique is a key to exquisiteness. Besides, the elegance and fascination of an exquisite work are always derived from its profound cultural content—spiritual assets such as history and traditions, faith, customs and habits or principles—which can be embodied by corresponding traditional or modern patterns or symbols.

Image ©ThinkBoldStudio!

ALMANAC GRAND CRU

-

studio

Chad Michael Studio

-

designer

Chad Michael

This is the 2016 limited edition bottle designed for Almanac Beer's annual Grand Cru Ales. The bottle is printed in 360 degrees with ceramic metallic inks. Each bottle is accompanied by a double foiled hang tag produced by letterpress printing.

As a kind of visual experience, what do you think about the "exquisiteness" in graphic design?

"Exquisite" to me is an all encompassing term for superior craftsmanship and intense attention to detail. Not every project calls for Exquisite, but when a project fits the criteria and an exquisite expression is expected, it should be done with a high level of authenticity, which will help develop brand identity and/or product story.

The choice of visual language a designer makes needs to make sense. Exquisiteness should neither be a compromise nor a go-to design solution that's used just for the sake of filling space. **The detailing, custom typography, and brilliant illustration that define exquisiteness need to be considered and hopefully do more than just look "pretty".** In terms of package design, if exquisiteness is correctly executed it should speak for not only the product within but also the price point, brand environment, and possibly the brand heritage.

NOMAD PLAYING CARDS

-

studio

Chad Michael Studio

-

designer

Chad Michael

NoMad Playing Cards were designed as a monument for The NoMad Hotel, which witnessed countless elite meetings in New York City in the 19th century. The design was inspired by the architectural elements of the hotel.

The back of the case resembles the shape of an eye, referring to the Latin phrase: "Beauty is in the eye of the beholder". With no detail left untouched, the result is a timeless blend of beauty and elegance.

What are your common approaches to produce an EXQUISITE visual effect?

I tend to follow a few key rules when achieving an exquisite look.

First and foremost I need to ensure that the design will be executed with customized ornamentation and typography, or at the very least heavily manipulated typography in order to make it ownable and applicable. One cannot produce a strong exquisite design with stock ornamentation and display typefaces, since they lack originality, which is the key to a satisfactory exquisite look.

Second, all aspects of the design need to make sense with the period or attitude that the product is intended to evoke. For example, if you are designing a Gin label of Scottish provenance, it needs to feel like it comes from Scotland. Every detail and typeface should evoke Scottish roots unless the concept demands otherwise. This is where historic and ephemeral research is imperative. That's why I strongly advise every designer to do the research! For example: the design should not feel Western unless it somehow makes sense for the brand's story. With every brand and product design, exquisite or not, the design should build a visual world for which it can live within. With every design choice, ask yourself, what does this say about the brand or product? Does this element help create a stronger design? If not, then keep exploring.

Third, the use of space. Even though an exquisite design is often full and illustrative, there should be balance and places for the eye to rest. A successful design, no matter how packed it is with detail, needs proper pacing so the eyes know how to navigate the work.

LUXURY PLAYING CARDS
CRAFTED IN THE UNITED STATES
FOR THE NOMAD HOTEL NYC
NORTH OF MADISON SQUARE
1170 BROADWAY
MADE IN THE UNITED STATES
· BY ·
Theory11
NOMAD
ESTABLISHED IN NEW YORK
TRADEMARK
LUXURY
PLAYING CARDS

THE 2017 ZBIGNIEW M. BIELAK ART CALENDAR

-

illustrator

Zbigniew M. Bielak

-

concept & designer

Joanna Tyborowska

The third edition of the annual Zbigniew M. Bielak Art Calendar—the daily planner—showcases over 53 original drawings and paintings by the polish artist and architect. Most of the illustrations were created as album artworks for a variety of rock and heavy metal bands, such as Ghost, Paradise Lost or Mayhem. Each spread contains one artwork and a weekly calendar, with holidays and multicultural observances marked alongside rock festivals. The lavish gold hot-stamped cover adds a luxurious feel so relevant to the aesthetics of music fan's collectables.

As a kind of visual experience, what do you think about the "exquisiteness" in graphic design?

The development of digital technology, has led to speculation that print, as a medium of information, will inevitably die. Though newspapers, brochures, and other short life-span content have been affected by this shift of power from paper to screen, enthusiasm predicting the decline of the print media seems premature.

In a world entangled with fast information and images vying for our attention, printed matter is synonymous with durability. When the battery runs out, physical products, especially those we refuse to throw away—the beautifully crafted tin can for expensive candies or the unique liquor bottle—will remain. We cherish the artifacts of these exquisite products, in such a way that the life of the product and its packaging design is prolonged. It is no surprise, that exclusive products, focusing on fine detailing, are in higher demand.

An exquisite design is a gift we give to others and a present we give to ourselves. **It is a treat that remind us not to rush.** It offers an out-of-the-ordinary moment that encourage us to savor every second.

WATAIN "LAWLESS DARKNESS" DOUBLE VINYL ALBUM

-

illustrator

Zbigniew M. Bielak

-

designer

Erik Danielsson

The collectors double vinyl edition of the fourth album of the Swedish black metal band Watain was designed as a statement against uninspired digital artworks, which were trending in the music scene at the time of its release. Opulently illustrated with fifteen hand drawings by Zbigniew M. Bielak, calligraphed by Timo Ketola, and designed as an elegant, triple gatefold, die-cut sleeve by the band's frontman Erik Danielsson, the album comes with a mounted booklet of artworks alongside song lyrics.

What are your common approaches to produce an EXQUISITE visual effect?

Contemporary trends in editorial design show a greater need, now than ever, to emphasize the sensory aspect of the designed work. While screens can generate endless virtual content at a speed that print can not manage, the coldness of the screen and limited sensory experience constrained to the eyes and ears, cannot compete with the natural appealing of touch and smell. The more memorable the sensory experience, the more exclusive and exquisite is the perception of such product.

Designing exquisite products, one is advised to concentrate on offering a sensory experience, which allows consumers to interact with the product in an intuitive way. **It is about engaging all senses and triggering emotional responses to the object.**

EXQUISITE means for designers to breed even the faintest finishing details—sometimes perceivable only through touch. The bespoke paper and texture, such as embossed matte and glossy surfaces, allow consumers to experience a sensory stimulate. And this, in a world filled with digital content, is a luxury.

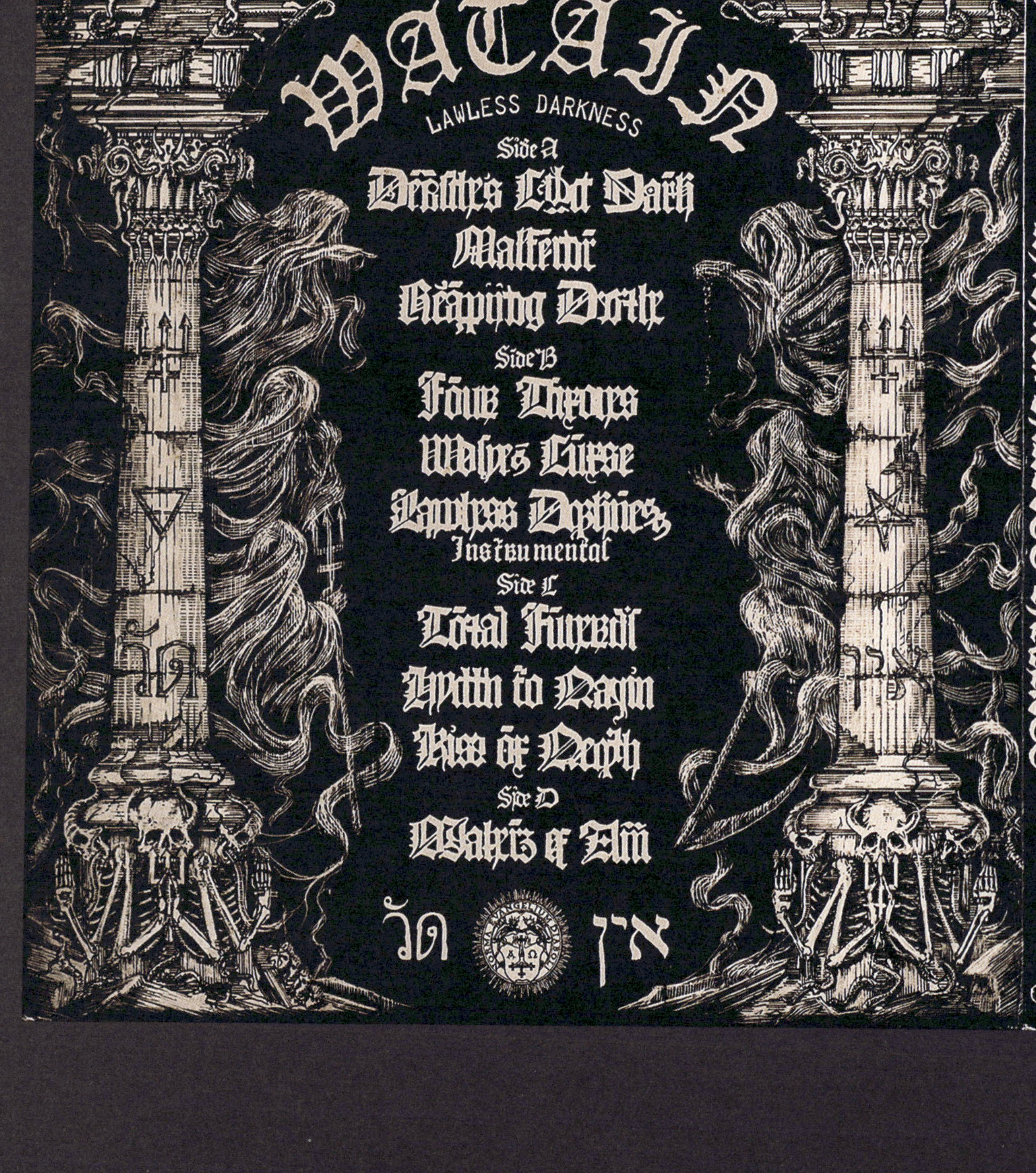
WATAIN
LAWLESS DARKNESS
Side A
Death's Cold Dark
Malfeitor
Reaping Death
Side B
Four Thrones
Wolves Curse
Lawless Darkness
Instrumental
Side C
Total Funeral
Hymn to Qayin
Kiss of Death
Side D
Waters of Ain
WATAIN: LAWLESS DARKNESS

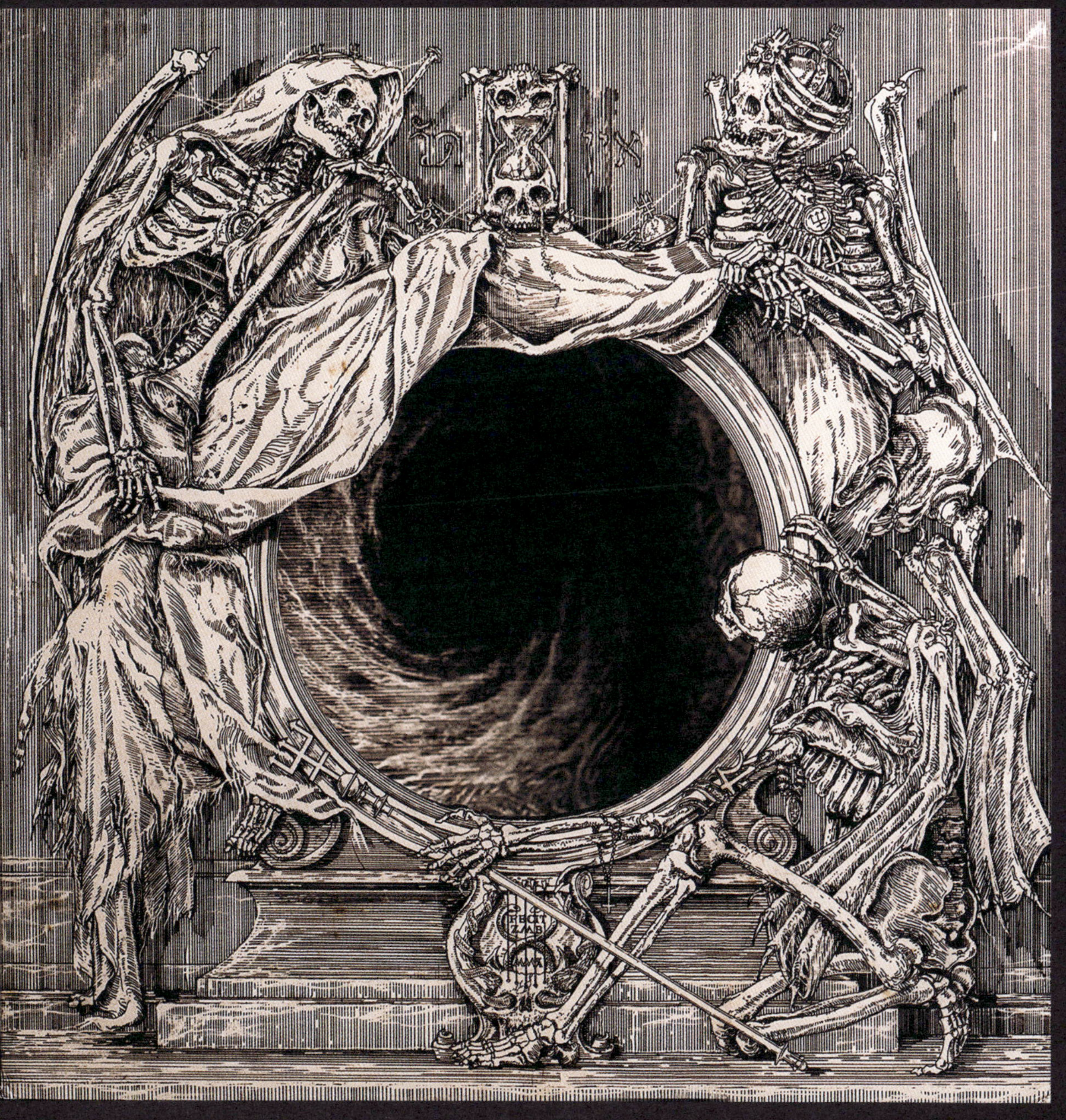

Flourish Playing Cards

This sweet new deck was inspired by the word "flourish". From the original pink back design to the illustrated court cards and custom faces, it is full of flavor. Like fine chocolate, the luxurious packaging is only a hint at the delectable cards inside. The gorgeous tuck case features foil and embossing on a rich paper to excite one's senses.

studio:
Column Five

designer:
Andrew Effendy

HIGH QUALITY PLAYING CARDS
MADE IN THE UNITED STATES OF AMERICA

HIGH QUALITY PLAYING CARDS

FRESHNESS
MAKER OF DELICIOUS DONUT AND PIE CHARTS
FRESHNESS

MAKER OF
DELICIOUS DONUT AND PIE CHARTS
HIGH QUALITY PLAYING CARDS
MADE IN THE UNITED STATES OF AMERICA

A
FLOURISHING
MADE IN U.S.A.
HIGH QUALITY PLAYING CARDS
MADE IN THE UNITED STATES OF AMERICA

FLOURISH
MAKER
OF
DELICIOUS

FLOURISH
MAKER
OF
DELICIOUS

Black Mama Craft Beer

Black Mama is a special edition black IPA craft beer, a result of the holistic connection between the process of making the beer and the crafting of the label. The design is characterized by the belief that the parts are intimately interconnected and accounted only by reference to the whole.

studio:

ThinkBoldStudio!

designer:

Hugo Marques

Black Mama
BY
ORIGINAL
1920

The Saint

The Saint is a chocolate stout made with Cacao from São Tomé. The gold foil and embossed printing, combined with intricate detail, gives a luxurious and stylish look to this craft beer.

studio:

ThinkBoldStudio!

designer:

Hugo Marques

CRAFT LOYAL
The
ESTD
Saint
2017
CHOCOLATE STOUT
by Pedro Sousa
CRAFT BEER
CHOCOLATE STOUT
CACAU DE SÃO TOMÉ
6,4%
ALC.VOL.

Sons of Liberty Playing Cards

Designed by Jeff Trish, produced by Art of Play and printed by the United States Playing Card Company, this traditional deck of 54 playing cards celebrates the founding of the United States of America. The Sons of Liberty was once a group who operated in the shadows and later won a widespread support to resist British oppression. This card deck takes you back to a time when they were subjects of a King across an ocean.

studio:
Art of Play

designer:
Jeff Trish

THE D&D PLAYING CARD CO.
DESIGNED BY JEFF TRISH

DESIGNED BY JEFF TRISH
FOR
THE D&D PLAYING CARD CO.

IS OBEDIENCE TO GOD

Emblossom

Inspired by Art Deco, the designers incorporated hand-drawn elements with beautiful typography to arrive at delicacy. To capture the feelings represented by the brand name "Emblossom", floral elements were added to the tail of the birds in the illustration. Black, white and gold have been chosen to express the identity.

studio:

MOJO DESIGN

designer:

Jay-tian

INVITATION
FROM EMBLOSSOM

EMBLOSSOM
THE
Emblossom
BAR | RESTAURANT | CAFE

VIP CARD
EMBLOSSOM

EMBLOSSOM

The Planets : Mercury

Mercury is a deck of cards featuring creatures with stone-like heat-resistant skin from the series Planets, a collection of decks representing the planets in solar system. The designers spent 9 months in creating this luxurious Vanda deck series focusing on every tiny detail.

studio:
Widakk Design

designer:
Srdjan Vidakovic

K
Q
J
K
Q
J

K
Q
J
K
Q
J

K
Q
J

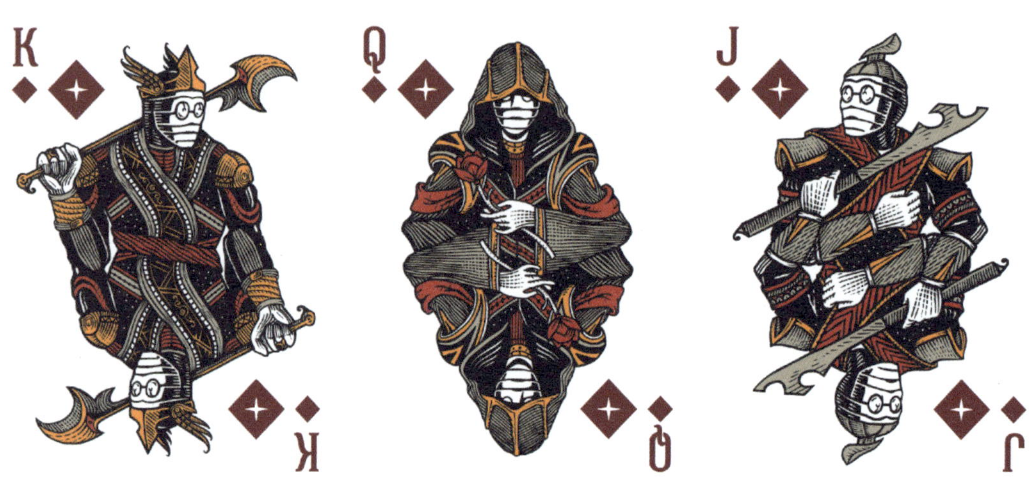
K
Q
J

JOKER
A
The
PLANETS
MERCURY
STELLAR PLAYING CARDS
A
JOKER

The
PLANETS
VANDA
VANDA ARTISTS SERIES
VANDACARDS.COM

Widakk
DESIGN
WIDAKK DESIGN
NOVI SAD SERBIA

Traditional Festival of Japan

This is a visual design for a Japanese traditional festival marked by a special gold ornament taikodai. Inspired by the breathtaking craftsmanship of the elaborate embroidery that decorated the taikodai, the designer incorporated gold leaf covering, Japanese calligraphy with modern design to reinterpret a scene from the myth, paying homage to the skilled craftsmen who contributed their delicate and bold embroidery to the ornamentation.

designer:

Yuta Takahashi

Mandarin Oriental Hong Kong Greetings Card

studio:
Happycentro

illustration & design:
Erica Zipoli

art director:
Federico Galvani

This is a limited edition greetings card for the renowned luxury hotel Hong Kong Mandarin Oriental to send to customers during winter festivities. The card depicts an imaginative port skyline incorporating architectural highlights of Hong Kong with Mandarin Oriental Hotel in the middle. The card was printed in letterpress using the amazing new Sumo white cardboard (3 mm thick, 2160 gsm) by Favini and it comes with a bespoke envelope hot stamped with gold foil, giving a terrific and clean effect.

Happy Holidays 2016

LP Record Cover

This LP record cover design was for *A Hard Days Night Treatment*. The foiling and printing were done in London.

designer:

Ben Johnston

SIDE A

1. A Hard Day's Night
2. There's a Place
3. Ticket to Ride
4. I'm Only Sleeping
5. Fixing a Hole
6. Norwegian Wood

SIDE B

1. Mother Nature's Son
2. I'll Follow the Sun
3. I Want to Hold your Hand
4. Flying
5. Golden Slumbers

5 060214 040365

ECC 100

A Hard Days Night Treatment

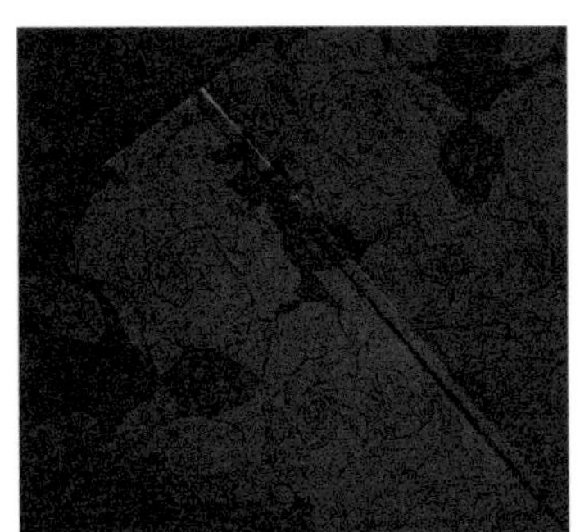

Convento Da Glória

Inspired by the splendor and exuberance of the Baroque style, this design renders a magical representation while reflecting the elegance of these wines. The label, with rich details that capture the essence and premium quality, invites viewers to travel to a time when monasteries, churches and palaces were enriched with unique gold decorative details. Gold embossed foil illustrations create an illusion of medieval illuminations with the capital letter "C" standing out. The background colors were chosen based on different grapes.

studio:

M&A Creative Agency

designer:

Maria Branco, Dalila Lopes

art director:
Carla Neves

creative director:
Luis Marques

photographer:
Igor Pinto , Pedro Oliveira

Well Bee Bhutan Honey

Well Bee is the name of the pure and natural honey products from Bhutan. The packaging design for this honey demonstrates great attention to detail. The motifs featured were inspired by traditional patterns of Thangkas—fascinating and exquisite paintings on fabric scrolls. The ornaments depicting landscape and vegetation of Bhutan refer to the colors of the four seasons. This sturdy wooden box is assembled by mortise and tenon joints, and can be reassembled according to different needs.

designer: *Yun-Xuan Wang, Sih-Ying Wang, Hui-Xue Chen, Wei-Lin Shie, Zheng-Cheng Ji, Chaoyang*

WELL
Bhutan's honey
BEE

WELL
BEE
WELL
BEE
WELL
BEE
WELL
BEE

WELL
BEE

WELL
honey
BEE

WELL
honey
BEE

JL Wedding Card

The wedding invitation design for Joshua and Liz was to be different from traditional wedding card designs. The designer integrates a western classical font and visual style with a modern layout design to illustrate the logo "JL", while developing a playful visual with star motifs and elements symbolizing love to show the belief held by the newly married couple.

J + L

designer:

Sean Huang

Tien
Syu
— Joshua & Liz —
SINCERELY INVITE
16 · 12 · 10
Tien & Syu
— FOREVER —

Xi Qin Rose Bible

This is a wedding cake and dessert packaging designed to cater for western-style weddings. The inspiration was from holy bible, and visual elements including lilies, roses, churches, wedding suits and bridal gowns are incorporated in the design.

designer:

Rory leichen

MOMENT 囍沁

WISHING YOU A WORLD OF HAPPINESS

LOVE AS ALL YOUR DREAMS COME TRUE

WEDDING

VOWS

FOR BETTER FOR WORSE

HAPPY WEDDING

LOVE FOREVER

WEDDING

·HAPPY WEDDING·

Grand Garden

The designers inherit the culture of Chinese garden and re-framed it into an exquisite tea packaging set. The packaging can be assembled by puzzle-like individual boxes, which contain all kinds of refreshments, tea leaves and tea set. Every delicate piece reveals an amazing scenery, recalling the excitement as one might have when encountering pleasing views in traditional Chinese garden. Consumers can disassemble and rearrange the combination to create their own imaginary Grand Garden.

designer:

Sung Cheng Jie, Lai Chih Ting

Synergy

This visual identity for the annual gathering of the most significant business partners of Primavera BSS took inspiration from Vidago Palace, a jewel from the Art Nouveau period and where the event would take place. The geometrical beauty of the Palace's skylight was considered to be perfectly in line with the visual language the designers were trying to deliver, and it served as the starting point to develop Synergy's identity that combine Art Nouveau with contemporary approach.

studio:
Pi Creative Studio

designer:
Pedro Matos

synergy
2016
synergy
2016
synergy
2016

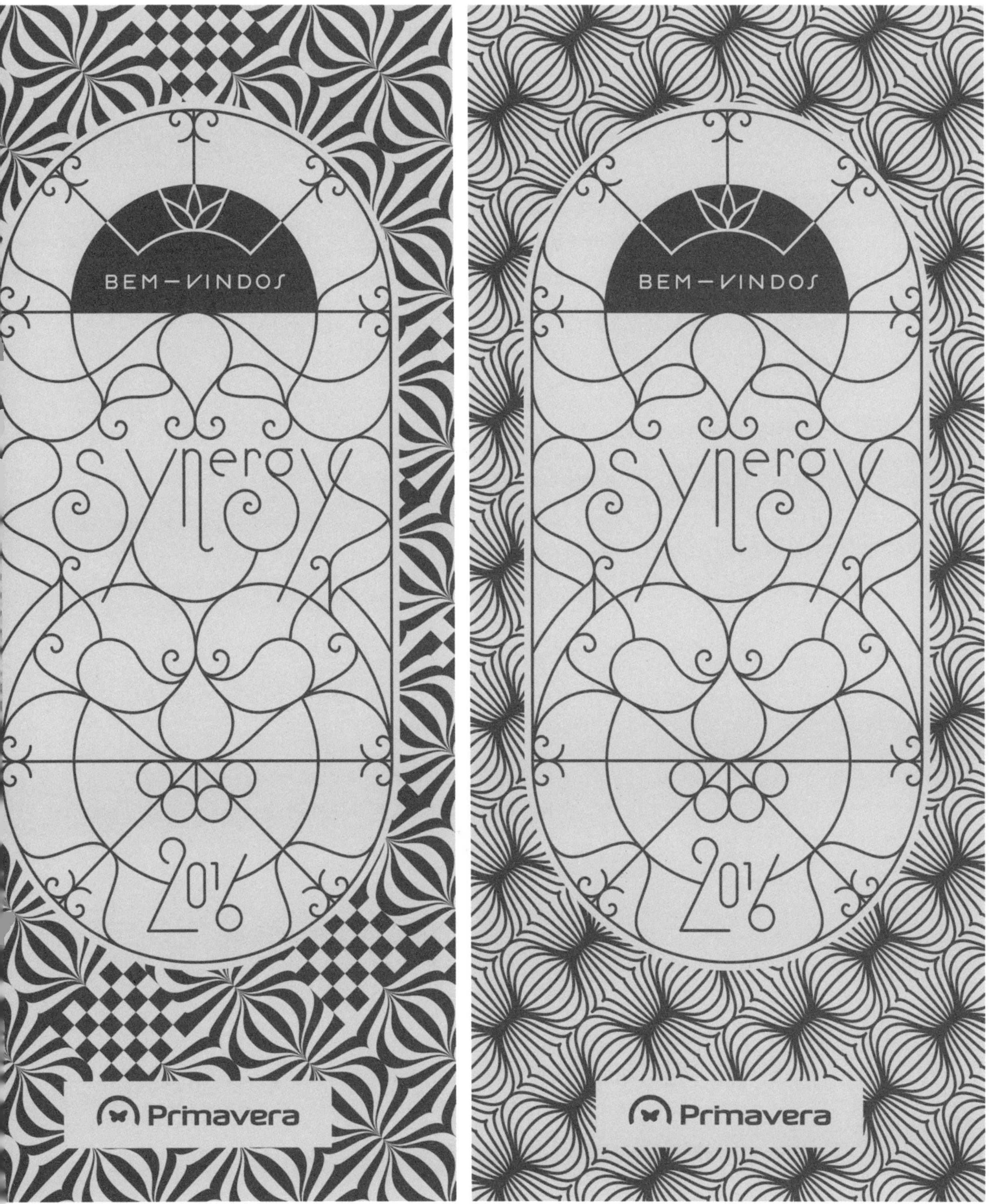
BEM-VINDOS
synergy
2016
Primavera
BEM-VINDOS
synergy
2016
Primavera

Terroir

Concept Brand Self-Promo

Sterling Creativeworks is an agency known for designing modern and classic packaging for wine, spirits and food. They developed a series of labels to expand client perception of what luxury wine packaging can look like when reinterpreting universal wine themes in unexpected ways.

The Terroir shares a new way to illustrate the vineyard, climate and soil.

studio:

Sterling Creativeworks

It's time for a new look at classic wine stories
No. 1 in a series of 4
The Visionist:
The winemaker as alchemist
Transforming simple fruit into a mystical
elixir. Harnessing the sun, soil, wind
and rain to enchant.
Which agency is behind this? Patience, my
friend, patience...
Enjoy the dark chocolate espresso beans
while you contemplate.
TERROIR
OF
NAPA VALLEY
CABERNET SAUVIGNON
WINEMAKER AS ALCHEMIST
GLASS · HANDLE WITH CARE
INVENTED HERITAGE

Nobility

Concept Brand
Self-Promo

Nobility riffs on the traditional label with an impish Bacchus crest, elegant flourishes and detailed embellishments.

studio:
Sterling Creativeworks

IN VINO
VERITAS
CARPE VINUM
NOBILITY
Cabernet Sauvignon
NAPA VALLEY
VINTED IN {2016} ANNO DOMINUS
MMXVI
1971

Notoriety

Concept Brand Self-Promo

Notoriety irreverently celebrates the spirit of a swashbuckling outlaw that lives in each of us. On the foil-embossed label depicts a fox stalking a wily rabbit — a known thief of wine grapes.

studio:

Sterling Creativeworks

NOTORIETY
VINTNERS

Visionist

Concept Brand
Self-Promo

The Visionist explores the winemaker's seemingly alchemical ability to create liquid poetry from simple grapes. Inspired by antique alchemy illustrations, the artwork for the label depicts the winemaker's magic.

studio:

Sterling Creativeworks

2016
vintage
NAPA VALLEY
THE
VISIONIST
CABERNET SAUVIGNON

Reynard

Reynard is a packaging design concept for a whiskey based on one of the oldest artefacts in Dutch literature—Van den vos Reynaerde. The chest containing the bottle looks like a piece of wood caught in a metal cage, implying the situation in which the protagonist red fox from the story gets caught, while the unique way it is opened refers to his cleverness. Each side of the chest has been engraved with images of other characters from the story.

designer:

Robbe Callewaert

REYNARD

Makers Playing Cards

Inspired by the many "makers" throughout mankind's history, Makers Playing Cards features 14 custom illustrated court cards representing the foundational makers that shaped the civilizations. It serves as a worldly tribute to these unique individuals and their contributions to humanity. Each tuck case has been embossed and stamped with layers of gold foil. A wood collector box was produced in a limited number of 300.

studio:
Chad Michael Studio

designer:
Chad Michael

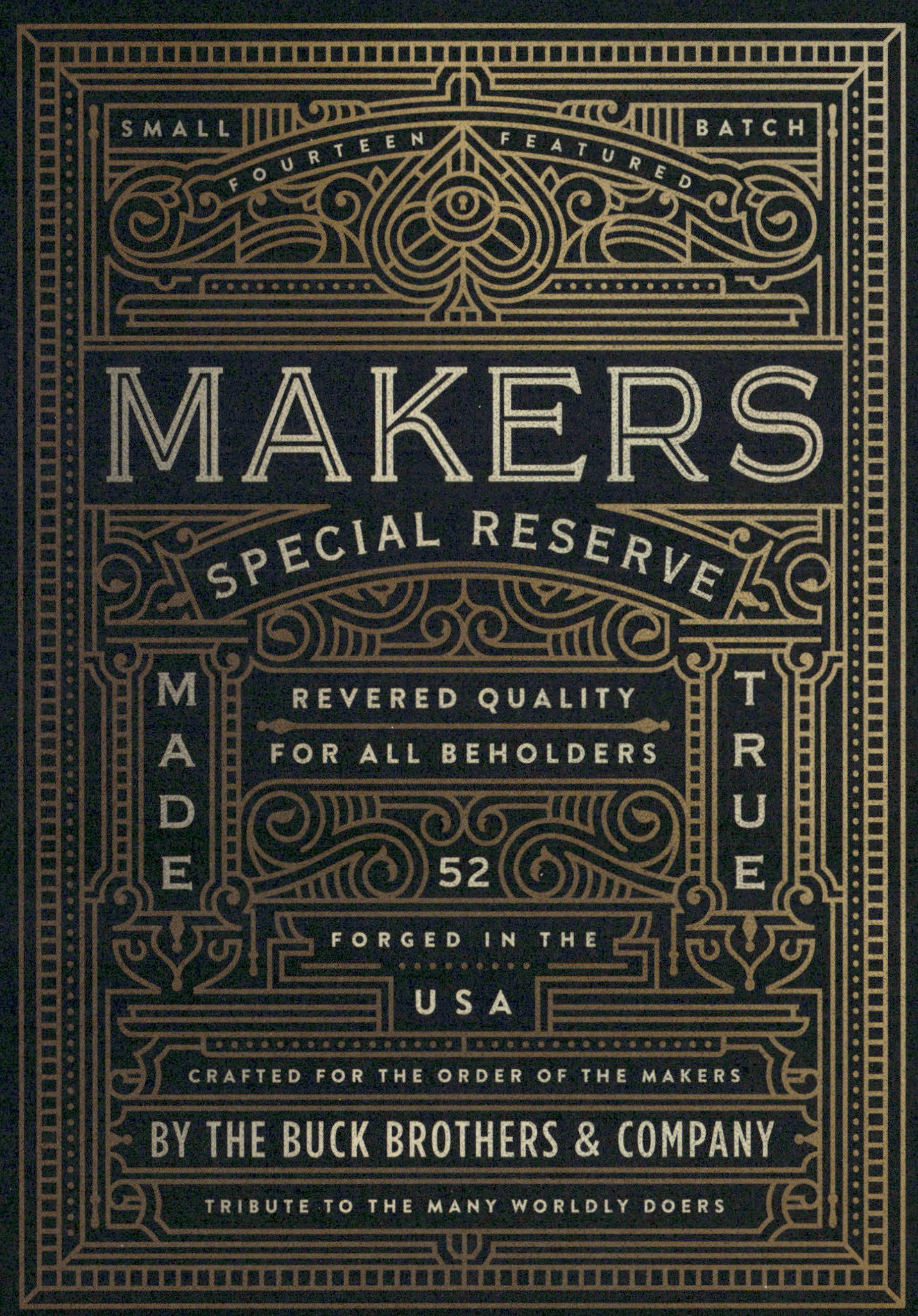
SMALL
BATCH
FOURTEEN FEATURED
MAKERS
SPECIAL RESERVE
MADE
TRUE
REVERED QUALITY
FOR ALL BEHOLDERS
52
FORGED IN THE
USA
CRAFTED FOR THE ORDER OF THE MAKERS
BY THE BUCK BROTHERS & COMPANY
TRIBUTE TO THE MANY WORLDLY DOERS

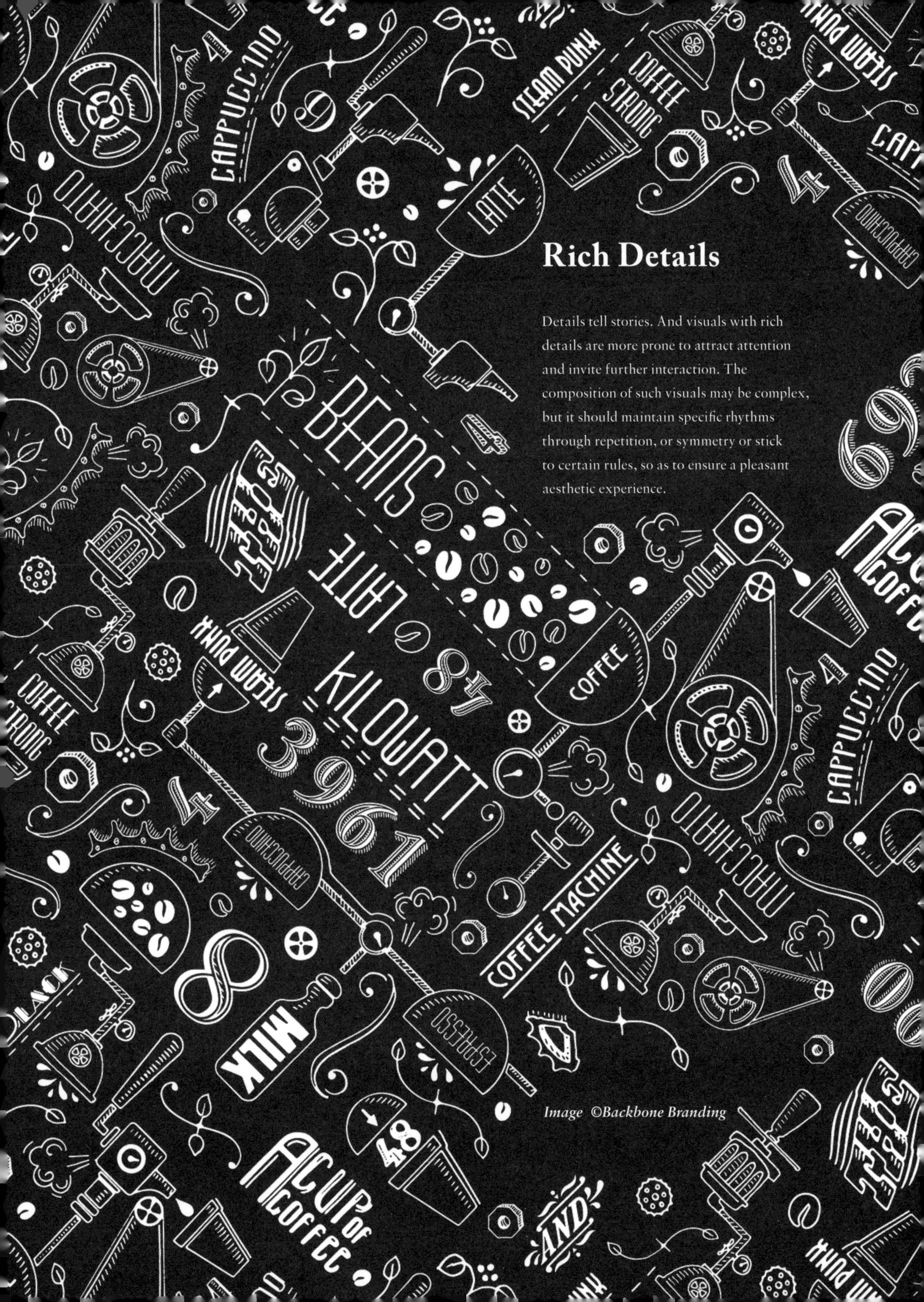

Rich Details

Details tell stories. And visuals with rich details are more prone to attract attention and invite further interaction. The composition of such visuals may be complex, but it should maintain specific rhythms through repetition, or symmetry or stick to certain rules, so as to ensure a pleasant aesthetic experience.

Image ©Backbone Branding

2644 HIGHLAND

-

studio

1983ASIA

-

designer

SUSU & YAO

After researching the spiritual belief and totem worship of local Mosuo, one of the only remaining matriarchal societies, 1983ASIA selected and refined the elements for a unique visual image of 2644 red rice. Modern techniques and materials were adopted to create the packaging with patterns referring to mountain and highland red rice, spreading the splendid Mosuo culture and its philosophy of returning to nature to a wider audience.

As a kind of visual experience, what do you think about the "exquisiteness" in graphic design?

An exquisite design is always the result of thoroughly digging into the theme and content and of genuine comprehension. The outcome will thrive with vitality with profound contemplation as its solid ground.

Exquisite designs offer an aesthetic pleasure with abundance of detail to peruse over time.

They concentrate designer's care, unique ideas and a large amount of time. **This dedication of attention, love, and patience represents an attitude that shall be cherished and encouraged.**

2644 HIGHLAND

FAIRTRADE
2644 HIGHLAND

2644 HIGHLAND

2644 HIGHLAND

What are your common approaches to produce an EXQUISITE visual effect?

We put great emphasis on making coherent and consistent designs. Therefore we give a lot of care to form and color; we care about their relationship with each other and their relationship with people. When a frame has been established, we will look into every detail, which is with so much fun. It is like preparing surprises for audience in advance.

Among the many ways to express exquisiteness, we like those traditional ones which involve skills with our hands and artistic abilities, such as drawing and painting with watercolor, color pencil, calligraphy or combining different devices. You can also incorporate modern techniques to produce exquisiteness, but there will be challenges. For example, the fineness of gold stamped lines or the requirement of combining different techniques, all should be treated with great care. All in all, we enjoy bringing the best together to push the boundary of our design to a new extreme.

FINDING HER UN WOMEN

-

Studio
IC4DESIGN Inc.

The three advertisements belongs to "Finding Her", a campaign preparation for the International Women's Day. These amazingly detailed pictures challenge audience to find the only woman in the scenes of three different workplaces: "Finding women in technology/politics/science shouldn't be this hard." The main objective behind the campaign was to highlight women's persistent low labor force participation rate and the importance of supporting an enabling environment with equal opportunities for women to reach their full potential.

As a kind of visual experience, what do you think about the "exquisiteness" in graphic design?

I think of exquisiteness as a feeling that will be evoked by meeting new combinations, new perspectives, and new discoveries in visual world. **It means beauty, but it also embodies the joy of touching new things.** For me, it is a miniature garden packed with feelings and dreams.

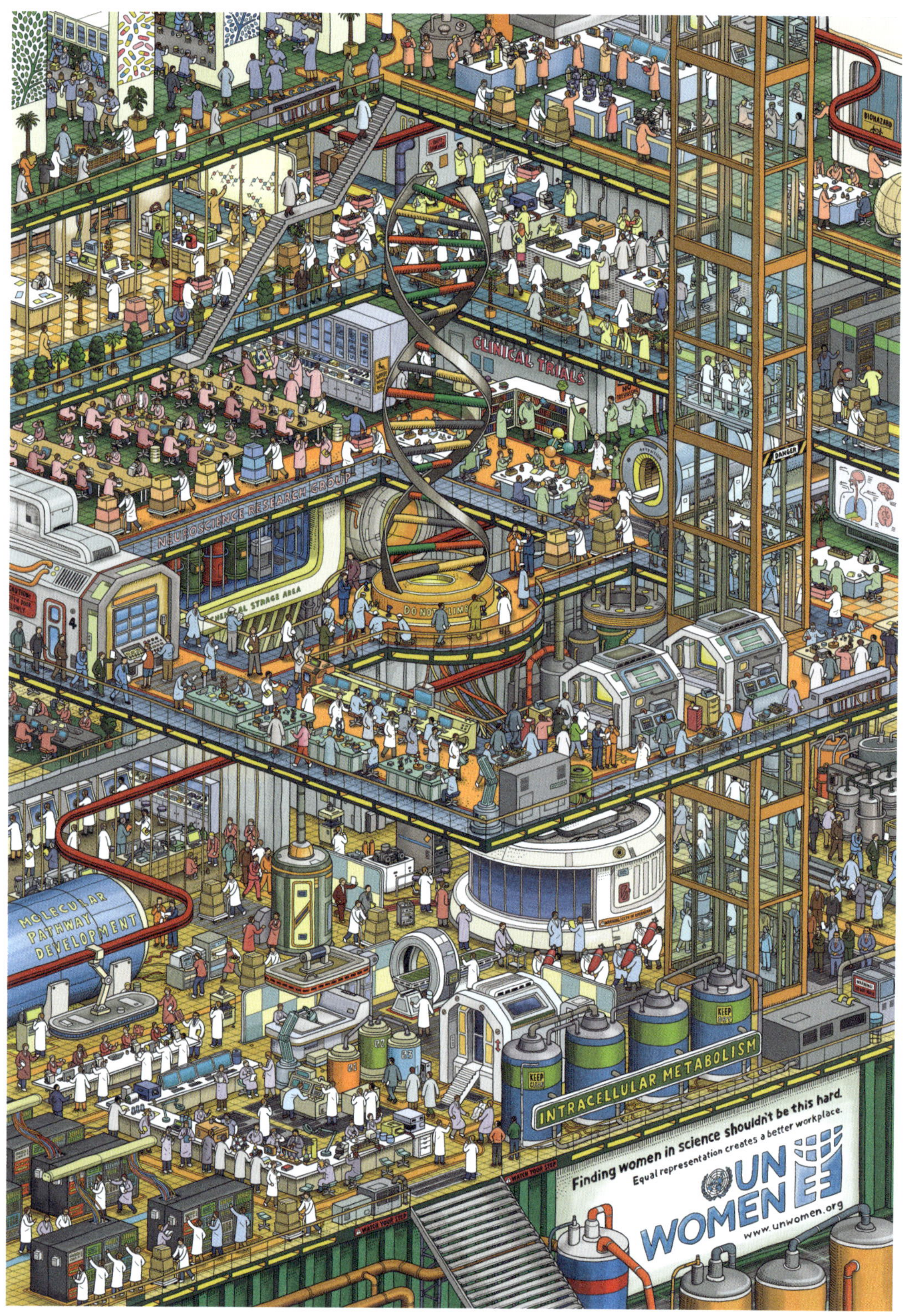
CLINICAL TRIALS
NEUROSCIENCE RESEARCH GROUP
DO NOT CLIMB
BIOHAZARD
DANGER
MOLECULAR PATHWAY DEVELOPMENT
KEEP DRY
INTRACELLULAR METABOLISM
Finding women in science shouldn't be this hard.
Equal representation creates a better workplace.
UN WOMEN
www.unwomen.org

What are your common approaches to produce an EXQUISITE visual effect?

It is to create a space and to build the miniature garden where I want to go, want to live in and want to fulfill my dreams. Usually I will begin my project from looking at my favourite photos and artworks, then I will browse through photos and illustrations on the subject before combining them together to form the idea. I will make a lot of small sketches as ideas brewing in my brain. In the execution of drawing, we will pay close attention to details. It is very often a time-consuming process, but I always draw with enjoyment and hope to share the feeling with whoever looks at my works.

EQUALITY
FREEDOM FOR ALL!
Finding women in politics shouldn't be this hard.
Equal representation creates a better workplace.
UN WOMEN
www.unwomen.org

KAEBISCH PACKAGING

-

studio

Mauro Martins

-

designer

Mauro Martins

Kaebisch is a Brazilian Chocolate brand now based in the US. They want to have a more impressive packaging for their Chocolate Bars. The intricate illustration printed over kraft paper tell stories about love for chocolate. Vibrant color stickers are placed over the box with product information.

As a kind of visual experience, what do you think about "Exquisite" in graphic design?

I think that "exquisite" is like a category in graphic design. It fits perfectly for some briefings, but not for all of them. **An exquisite design, if used properly, will add value to the product and make it more interesting and charming.** On the other hand, if the briefing expects a reinforcement of some specific product features like cheap price for example, then, in my opinion, an exquisite design would not match accordingly. Choosing the right visual language plays a big role for any design projects. Personally, I love attending assignments where an exquisite language is welcome.

TASTILLERY PACKAGING

-

designer

Mauro Martins, Waldemar Wegelin

For Tastillery, a product all about discovery, the designers decided that the packaging should be the first step of this discovery and the box itself should make people curious and get them ready for inspiration. Sitting down and imagining all kinds of drinking situations including the real and the surreal, the designers made a decision to combine hundreds of stories into one giant illustration in Mauro's style. The end result is an entertaining box which is a part of the drinking experience.

What are your common approaches to produce an EXQUISITE visual effect?

To reach an exquisite style, I like using reduced color palettes. **Here, less is more.** This is not only the case with colors, but also with graphic elements. Even though my illustration style is complex itself, at the end the whole system can work out like a simple texture and the illustration be pretty much the only graphic element besides the logo and text. Using resources like foil, special colors and nice dielines can also help achieve an exquisite visual expression.

An Amulet Against Spam Mail

Based on the idea that perhaps people were put under a spell to encounter masses of spam that go through all means to catch everyone's attention every day, the designer created a spiritual amulet to prevent people from deception. The piece consists of a book containing an amulet for possession and duplication, and instructions to using the amulet.

designer:

Jungeun Choi

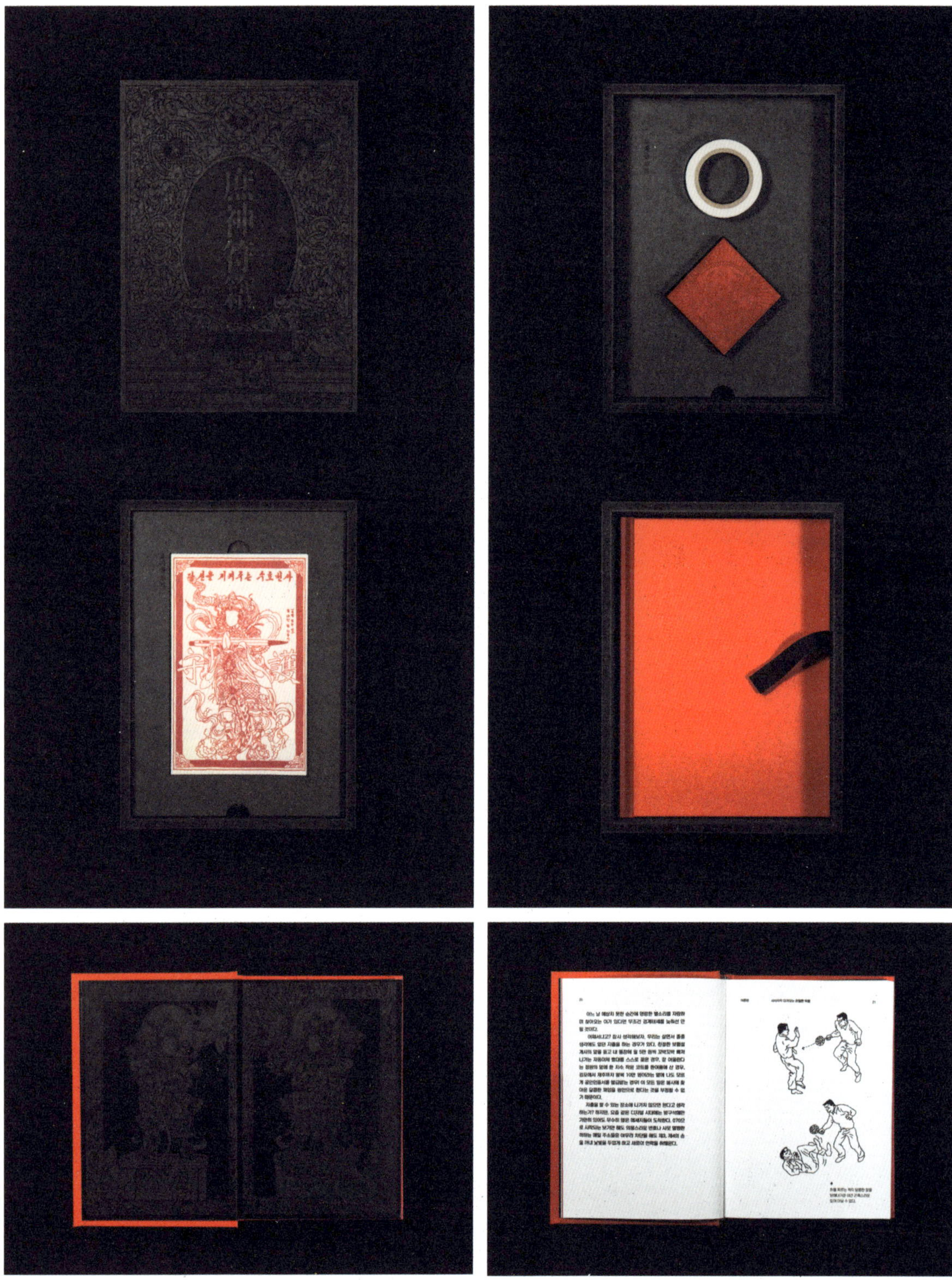

당신을 지켜주는 수호천사
守護

축하합니다

김미영 팀장입니다.
김미영

오빠, 나 기억할련지 모르겠다...

Episode IV Mandala

The designer has made a mandala centered around the ships in *Star Wars Episode IV: A New Hope* with amazing details.

designer:

Tony Bamber

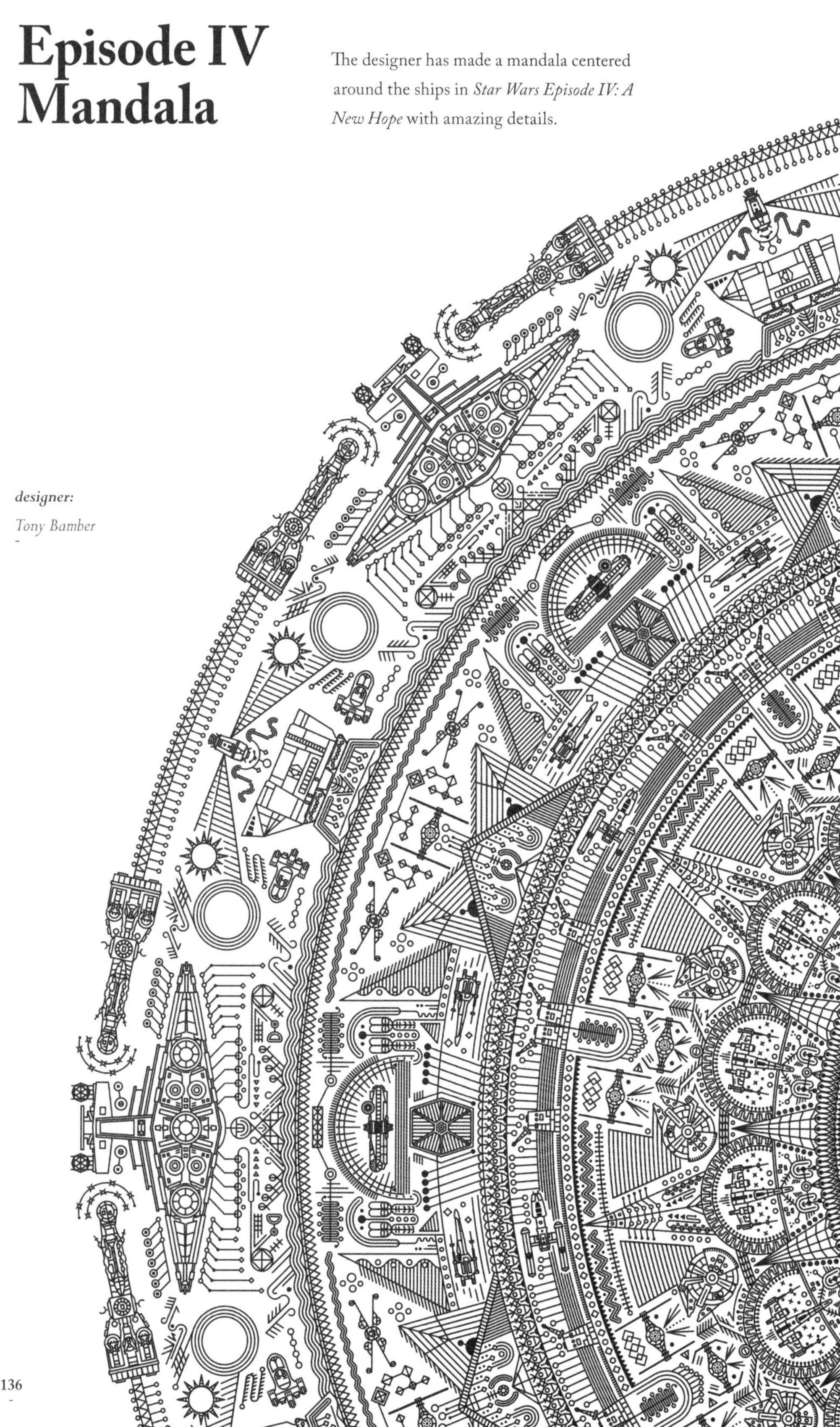

The Fairytale Collection

To reinterpret the Hans Christian's universe, Bessermachen Design Studio created the Fairytale Collection featuring 9 wonderful chocolate bars based on the fairy tales. The inspiration for both the design and the chocolate was from the fairy tales, which are all about betrayal, greed, overweening ambition and love and are still captivating and fascinating for modern eyes. Sharing the same passion for a great story, the studio sees the stories as an open book for understanding the essence of Denmark.

studio:
Bessermachen Design studio

designer:
Kristin Brandt

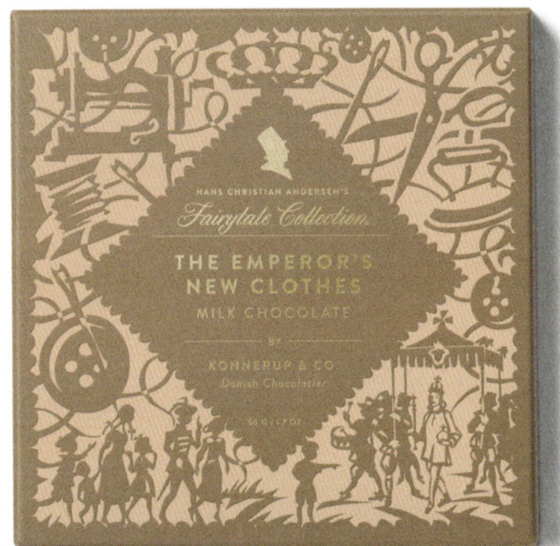

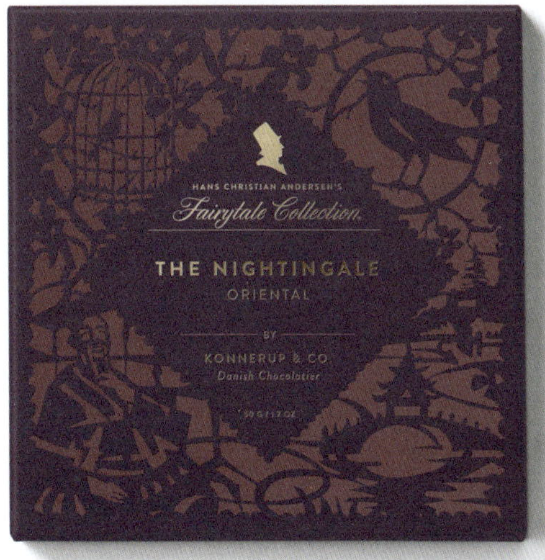

illustrator:

Niels Ditlev

HANS CHRISTIAN ANDERSEN'S
Fairytale Collection
THE SNOW QUEEN
WHITE CHOCOLATE
BY
KONNERUP & CO.
Danish Chocolatier
50 G / 1.7 OZ

HANS CHRISTIAN ANDERSEN'S
Fairytale Collection
THUMBELINA
DARK LAVENDER
BY
KONNERUP & CO.
Danish Chocolatier
50 G / 1.7 OZ

QCSHS 50th Anniversary Book Cover

These illustrations were created for the limited-edition commemorative coffee table book to celebrate the 50th anniversary of Quezon City Science High School. Using the school's motto "Scientia Et Virtus" (Latin for "Knowledge and Virtue") as inspiration, the illustrations are meant to resemble a vintage timepiece that records all of the school's achievements in science education.

designer:

Samuel Leon

1967
NATURAL
SOCIAL
QUEZON CITY SCIENCE HIGH SCHOOL
SCIENTIA
ET
VIRTUS
Golden Anniversary
NATIONAL
CAPITAL REGION
ESTABLISHED MCMLXVII
FORMAL
APPLIED
2017

The New Moscow Map

Since the New Moscow directed attention to Constructivist architecture including 180 buildings and housing estates located within the ring road, a map showing unknown as well as world famous buildings in constructivist style was drawn. Many of these buildings, often seen as reminders of the country's communist past and regarded as cheap and ugly by the public, are falling into disrepair and risk of demolition. Thus the creation of this map is to highlight the architectural significance of these buildings and to ensure their preservation.

studio:
Baklazanas Design studio

designer:
Irina Goryacheva

87
86
3-Й КРУТИЦКИЙ ПЕР.
НОВОСПАССКИЙ ПР-Д
90
94
95
96
92

ПЕТРОВСКИЙ Б-Р
РОЖДЕСТВЕНСКИЙ
Б. ДМИТРОВКА
ПЕТРОВКА
НЕГЛИННАЯ
РОЖДЕСТВЕНКА
ЛУБЯНКА
5
7
ТЕАТРАЛЬН. ПР-Д
НОВАЯ ПЛ.
КРАСНАЯ ПЛ.
2
ИЛЬИНКА
ВАСИЛЬЕВ. С.
ЛЕНИН
ВАРВАРКА
1
16

ВСЕМ..
ВСЕМ..
ВСЕМ..
НОВАЯ
Москва
2016
КАРТА КОНСТРУКТИВИСТСКОЙ МОСКВЫ
ВСЕМ..
ВСЕМ..
ВСЕМ..

ВСЕМ..
ВСЕМ..
ВСЕМ..
Новая
Москва
2016
КАРТА КОНСТРУКТИВИСТСКОЙ МОСКВЫ
ВСЕМ..
ВСЕМ..
ВСЕМ..
МКАД

Postcards For Morshyn City

This series of postcards for Morshyn city in Ukraine features stylish patterns of tree of life symbolizing the source of health. The designer presents traditional Ukrainian ornaments in a modern style with twelve unique illustrations, the colors of which correspond with different times of the year.

concept:
Mariia Fozekosh

designer:
Kate Iatsushek

Моршин – джерело здоров'я

Моршин – джерело здоров'я

Моршин – джерело здоров'я

Моршин – джерело здоров'я

Моршин – джерело здоров'я

Моршин – джерело здоров'я

Моршин – джерело здоров'я

Моршин – джерело здоров'я

Моршин – джерело здоров'я

The Astrozodiac Calendar

The Astrozodiac Calendar is based on Josef Manes's calendar located under Prague's Astronomical Clock, which depicts the twelve zodiac signs alongside rural life scenes in Prague. This work features a redesign of the twelve zodiac signs alongside illustrations representing ancient Greek mythology and mythological creatures. The numbering in the calendar indicates the moon's phases of the year. The central element features a sun based on ancient Greek drama masks aligned with the mythological style. The general layout and the typography refer to the Art Nouveau style.

studio:

Corn Studio

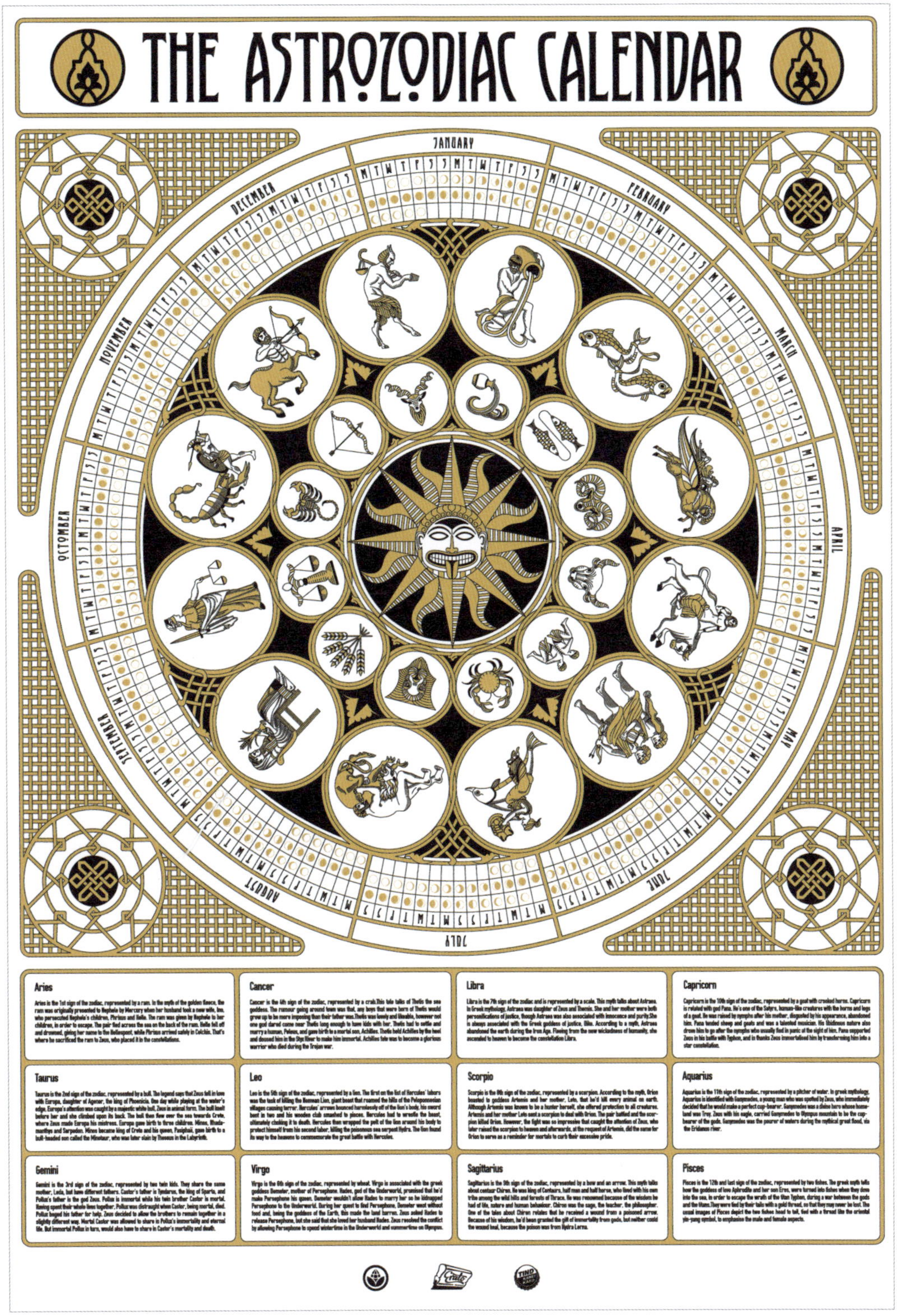

THE ASTROZODIAC CALENDAR

JANUARY · FEBRUARY · MARCH · APRIL · MAY · JUNE · JULY · AUGUST · SEPTEMBER · OCTOBER · NOVEMBER · DECEMBER

Aries

Aries is the 1st sign of the zodiac, represented by a ram. In the myth of the golden fleece, the ram was originally presented to Nephele by Mercury when her husband took a new wife, Ino, who persecuted Nephele's children, Phrixus and Helle. The ram was given by Nephele to her children, in order to escape. The pair fled across the sea on the back of the ram. Helle fell off and drowned, giving her name to the Hellespont, while Phrixus arrived safely in Colchis. That's where he sacrificed the ram to Zeus, who placed it in the constellations.

Taurus

Taurus is the 2nd sign of the zodiac, represented by a bull. The legend says that Zeus fell in love with Europa, daughter of Agenor, the king of Phoenicia. One day while playing at the water's edge, Europa's attention was caught by a majestic white bull, Zeus in animal form. The bull knelt before her and she climbed upon its back. The bull then flew over the sea towards Crete, where Zeus made Europa his mistress. Europa gave birth to three children, Minos, Rhadamanthys and Sarpedon. Minos became king of Crete and his queen, Pasiphaë, gave birth to a bull-headed son called the Minotaur, who was later slain by Theseus in the Labyrinth.

Gemini

Gemini is the 3rd sign of the zodiac, represented by two twin kids. They share the same mother, Leda, but have different fathers. Castor's father is Tyndarus, the king of Sparta, and Pollux's father is the god Zeus. Pollux is immortal while his twin brother Castor is mortal. Having spent their whole lives together, Pollux was distraught when Castor, being mortal, died. Pollux begged his father for help. Zeus decided to allow the brothers to remain together in a slightly different way. Mortal Castor was allowed to share in Pollux's immortality and eternal life. But immortal Pollux in turn, would also have to share in Castor's mortality and death.

Cancer

Cancer is the 4th sign of the zodiac, represented by a crab.This tale talks of Thetis the sea goddess. The rumour going around town was that, any boys that were born of Thetis would grow up to be more imposing than their father was.Thetis was lovely and likeable, however not one god dared come near Thetis long enough to have kids with her. Thetis had to settle and marry a human, Peleus, and gave birth to a mortal son, Achilles. Thetis held Achilles by the heel and doused him in the Styx River to make him immortal. Achilles fate was to become a glorious warrior who died during the Trojan war.

Leo

Leo is the 5th sign of the zodiac, represented by a lion. The first on the list of Hercules' labors was the task of killing the Nemean Lion, giant beast that roamed the hills of the Peloponnesian villages causing terror. Hercules' arrows bounced harmlessly off of the lion's body, his sword bent in two and his wooden club smashed to pieces. Hercules had to wrestle the beast, ultimately choking it to death. Hercules then wrapped the pelt of the lion around his body to protect himself from his second labor, killing the poisonous sea serpent Hydra. The lion found its way to the heavens to commemorate the great battle with Hercules.

Virgo

Virgo is the 6th sign of the zodiac, represented by wheat. Virgo is associated with the greek goddess Demeter, mother of Persephone. Hades, god of the Underworld, promised that he'd make Persephone his queen. Demeter wouldn't allow Hades to marry her so he kidnapped Persephone to the Underworld. During her quest to find Persephone, Demeter went without food and, being the goddess of the Earth, this made the land barren. Zeus asked Hades to release Persephone, but she said that she loved her husband Hades. Zeus resolved the conflict by allowing Persephone to spend wintertime in the Underworld and summertime on Olympus.

Libra

Libra is the 7th sign of the zodiac and is represented by a scale. This myth talks about Astraea. In Greek mythology, Astraea was daughter of Zeus and Themis. She and her mother were both personifications of justice, though Astraea was also associated with innocence and purity.She is always associated with the Greek goddess of justice, Dike. According to a myth, Astraea abandoned the earth during the Iron Age. Fleeing from the new wickedness of humanity, she ascended to heaven to become the constellation Libra.

Scorpio

Scorpio is the 8th sign of the zodiac, represented by a scorpion. According to the myth, Orion boasted to goddess Artemis and her mother, Leto, that he'd kill every animal on earth. Although Artemis was known to be a hunter herself, she offered protection to all creatures. Artemis and her mother Leto sent a scorpion to deal with Orion. The pair battled and the scorpion killed Orion. However, the fight was so impressive that caught the attention of Zeus, who later raised the scorpion to heaven and afterwards, at the request of Artemis, did the same for Orion to serve as a reminder for mortals to curb their excessive pride.

Sagittarius

Sagittarius is the 9th sign of the zodiac, represented by a bow and an arrow. This myth talks about centaur Chiron. He was king of Centaurs, half man and half horse, who lived with his own tribe among the wild hills and forests of Thrace. He was renowned because of the wisdom he had of life, nature and human behaviour. Chiron was the sage, the teacher, the philosopher. One of the tales about Chiron relates that he received a wound from a poisoned arrow. Because of his wisdom, he'd been granted the gift of immortality from gods, but neither could the wound heal, because the poison was from Hydra Lerna.

Capricorn

Capricorn is the 10th sign of the zodiac, represented by a goat with crooked horns. Capricorn is related with god Pana. He's one of the Satyrs, human-like creatures with the horns and legs of a goat. He was raised by nymphs after his mother, disgusted by his appearance, abandoned him. Pana tended sheep and goats and was a talented musician. His libidinous nature also drove him to go after the nymphs who usually fled in panic at the sight of him. Pana supported Zeus in his battle with Typhon, and in thanks Zeus immortalised him by transforming him into a star constellation.

Aquarius

Aquarius is the 11th sign of the zodiac, represented by a pitcher of water. In greek mythology, Aquarius is identified with Ganymedes, a young man who was spotted by Zeus, who immediately decided that he would make a perfect cup-bearer. Ganymedes was a divine hero whose homeland was Troy. Zeus with his eagle, carried Ganymedes to Olympus mountain to be the cup-bearer of the gods. Ganymedes was the pourer of waters during the mythical great flood, via the Eridanus river.

Pisces

Pisces is the 12th and last sign of the zodiac, represented by two fishes. The greek myth tells how the goddess of love Aphrodite and her son Eros, were turned into fishes when they dove into the sea, in order to escape the wrath of the titan Typhon, during a war between the gods and the titans.They were tied by their tails with a gold thread, so that they may never be lost. The usual images of Pisces depict the two fishes head to tail, tied with a thread like the oriental yin-yang symbol, to emphasise the male and female aspects.

Stamp Design for Hungarian Folk Tales

This stamp series design stemmed from designer's discovery that there was no stamp series emphasizing the Hungarian folk tales even though some tale-themed stamps exist in Hungary. With a keen interest in folk tales, the designer made this series for her degree project, and more importantly, as a pleasant creation to deliver joy to a wider range of audience.

designer:

Boglárka Nádi

PREMIER JOUR
ELSŐ NAP
FIRST DAY
SOPRON
2012.VI.06.

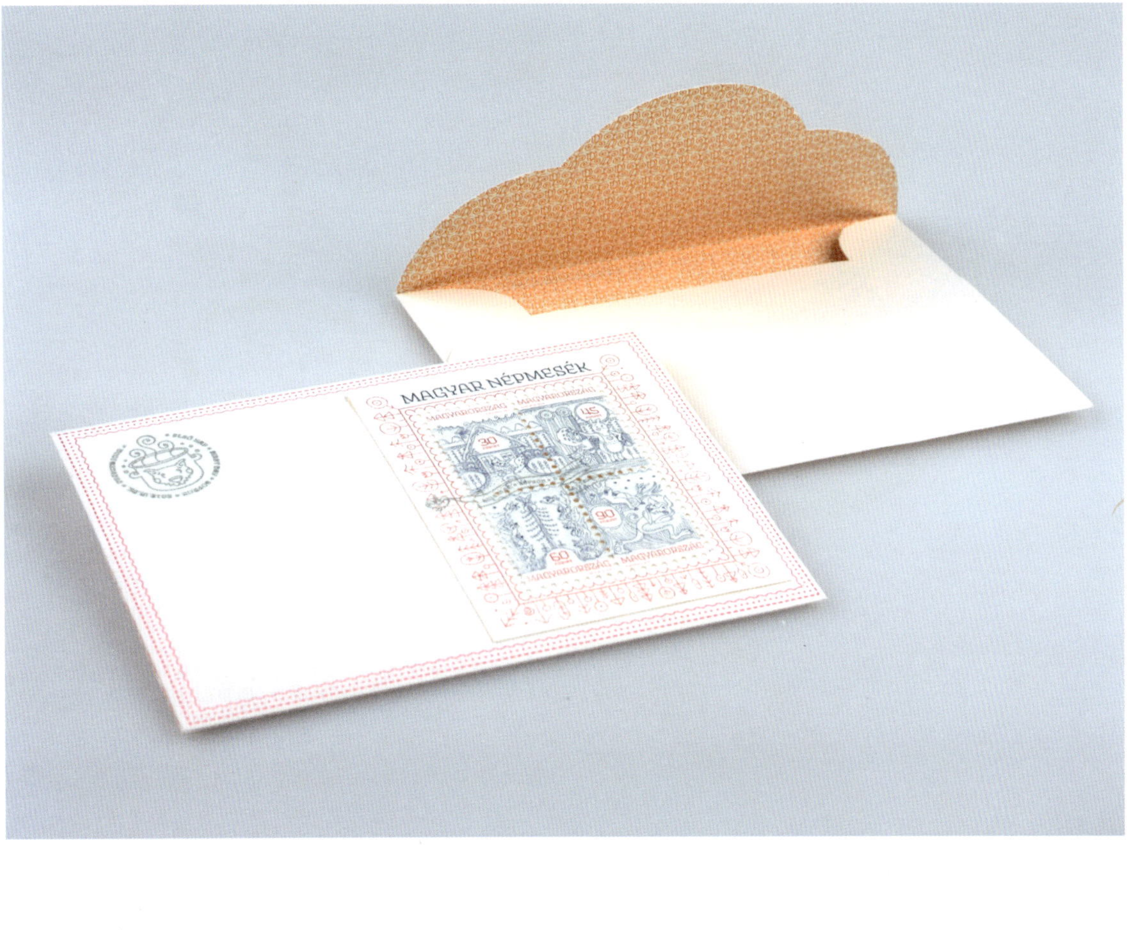

MAGYAR NÉPMESÉK
MAGYARORSZÁG
MAGYARORSZÁG
30
FORINT
45
FORINT
90
FORINT
60
FORINT
MAGYARORSZÁG
MAGYARORSZÁG

MAGYAR NÉPMESÉK
MAGYARORSZÁG
MAGYARORSZÁG
30
FORINT
45
FORINT
60
FORINT
90
FORINT
MAGYARORSZÁG
MAGYARORSZÁG

MAGYAR NÉPMESÉK
MAGYARORSZÁG
MAGYARORSZÁG
30
FORINT
45
FORINT
90
FORINT
60
FORINT
MAGYARORSZÁG
MAGYARORSZÁG

MAGYAR NÉPMESÉK
MAGYARORSZÁG
MAGYARORSZÁG
30 FORINT
45 FORINT
90 FORINT
60 FORINT
MAGYARORSZÁG
MAGYARORSZÁG

MAGYAR NÉPMESÉK
MAGYARORSZÁG
MAGYARORSZÁG
30 FORINT
45 FORINT
60 FORINT
90 FORINT
MAGYARORSZÁG
MAGYARORSZÁG

MAGYAR NÉPMESÉK
MAGYARORSZÁG
MAGYARORSZÁG
45 FORINT
30 FORINT
60 FORINT
90 FORINT
MAGYARORSZÁG
MAGYARORSZÁG

Blue &White Porcelain Playing Cards

Inspired by traditional Chinese blue and white porcelain; this deck features hand-painted and digitally refined illustrations that depict the twelve animals of the Chinese zodiac system. Decorative motifs and a clean aesthetic seen in the deck also draw influence from contemporary Scandinavian ceramics. By combining the two different styles harmoniously, the design suggests a fusion of the East and the West.

designer:

Shann Larsson

K
Q
J
K
Q
J

Muuk

For Incas and Aztecs, quinoa, amaranth and Chia seeds are power-food more valuable than gold due to their healthy ingredients and nutritional value. Based on this concept, a packaging shaped like a gold bar has been created. Through magnetic latches it could be folded into different forms, delivering different functions. The patterns are related to Inca or Aztec' culture while the name "MUUK" means "strength" in Yucatec, a Mayan language.

studio:
bungalow kreativbüro

designer:
Yvonne Moser

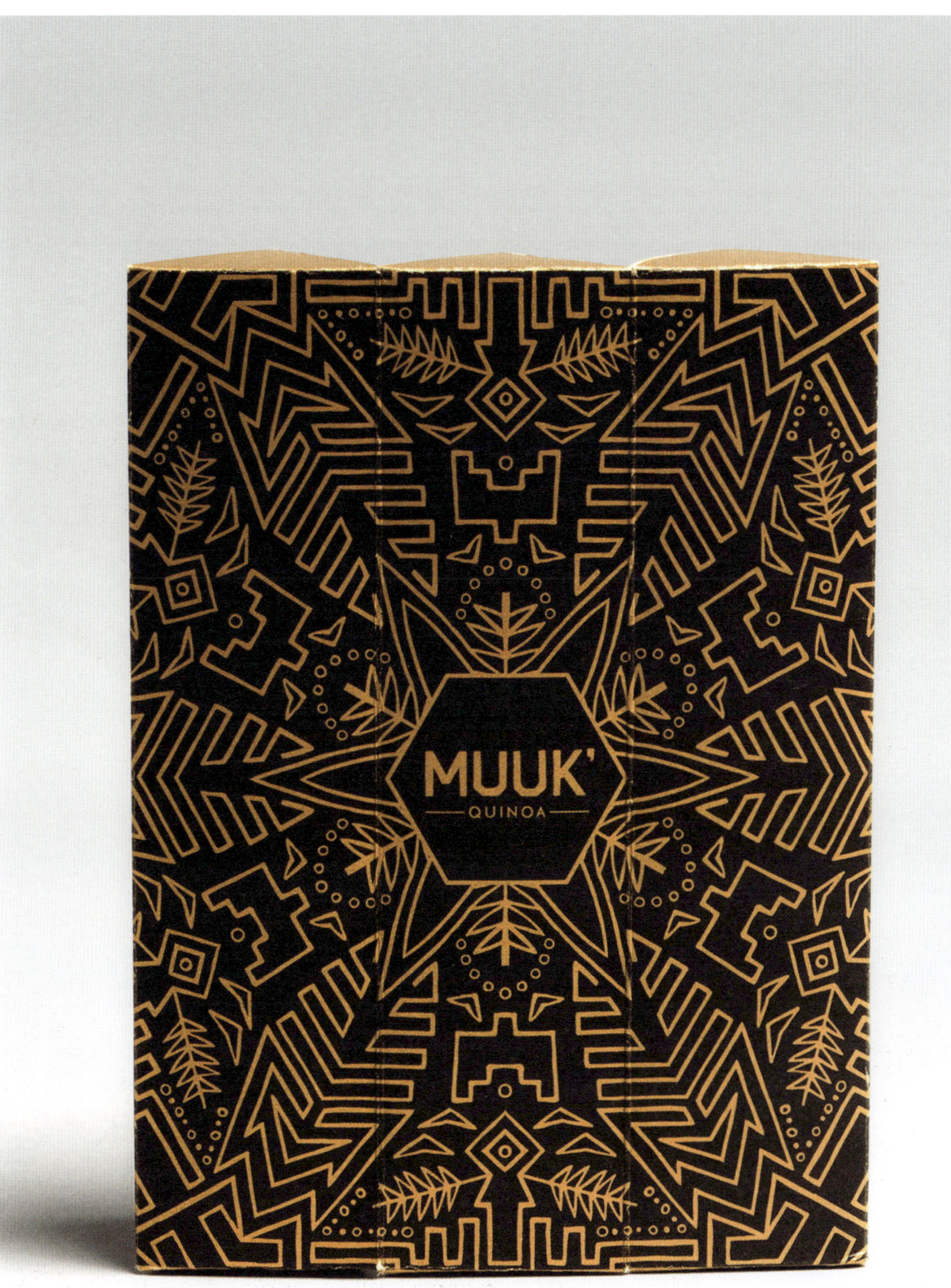
MUUK'
QUINOA

Metropolis

Metropolis is a thematic bazaar concept that presents vendors from the fields of fashion, lifestyle, food and also workshops. This bazaar is conceptualized and visually designed to bring the glamorous magnetism of the Gatsby-era which is strongly influenced by Art Deco movement. The name Metropolis is taken from the futuristic city, wealthy industrialist reign marked by high-rise towering complexes.

designer:

Dhimas Zoso

HIVE by Milestone
METROPOLIS

Jameson Irish Whiskey

Deconstrusted Series

Designer Greg Coulton was commissioned by design agency Pond Sweden to design and illustrate the new, super-premium Jameson "Deconstructed Series". The goal was to capture the character and personality of each whiskey in a unique and captivating narrative. Intensely detailed, multi-layered and hand crafted, each illustration perfectly embodies the whiskey it adorns.

studio:
Greg Coulton

designer:
Greg Coulton

art director:

Cecilia Bjare

JAMESON®
JAMESON®
Established
Since 1780
SINE METU
LIVELY
ELEGANT & FLORAL WITH CITRUSY LIGHTNESS. LIKE A SOFT BREEZE
Triple Distilled
IRISH WHISKEY
PRODUCT OF IRELAND
THE BOW ST. DISTILLERY
DUBLIN 7, IRELAND
40% vol.
1Litre ℮
JAMESON ORIGINAL'S KEY CHARACTERISTICS PULLED APART & AMPLIFIED

JAMESON
JAMESON
JAMESON
Established Since 1780
SINE METU
ROUND
RICH & RIPE WITH TOASTED WOOD TONES. BALANCED TO PERFECTION
Triple Distilled
IRISH WHISKEY
PRODUCT OF IRELAND
THE BOW ST. DISTILLERY
DUBLIN 7, IRELAND
40% vol.
1Litre e
JAMESON ORIGINAL'S KEY CHARACTERISTICS PULLED APART & AMPLIFIED

Pay It Forward

This piece was set out to be a unique gift for clients. It captures the spirit of the values upheld by its creator and inspires greater good. The inspiration was from a beautifully written letter by Benjamin Franklin that told the pay-it-forward philosophy. A poster based on the letter featuring modern typography, illustration and design style was created, and the final design was brought to life by hot-stamping copper foil on colored papers.

studio:
Column Five

designer:
Andrew Effendy

DEAR SIR,
I RECEIVED YOURS OF THE 15TH INSTANT, AND THE MEMORIAL IT INCLOSED.
THE ACCOUNT THEY GIVE OF YOUR SITUATION GRIEVES ME.
I SEND YOU HEREWITH A BILL FOR TEN LOUIS D'ORS.
I DO NOT PRETEND TO GIVE SUCH A SUM; I ONLY LEND IT TO YOU.
WHEN YOU SHALL RETURN TO YOUR COUNTRY WITH A GOOD CHARACTER,
YOU CANNOT FAIL OF GETTING INTO SOME BUSINESS, THAT WILL IN TIME ENABLE YOU TO PAY ALL YOUR DEBTS.
IN THAT CASE, WHEN YOU MEET
WITH
ANOTHER HONEST MAN IN SIMILAR DISTRESS,
YOU MUST PAY ME
BY
LENDING THIS SUM TO HIM;
ENJOINING HIM
TO DISCHARGE THE DEBT
BY
A LIKE OPERATION,
WHEN HE SHALL BE ABLE,
AND SHALL MEET
WITH
ANOTHER OPPORTUNITY.
I HOPE IT MAY THUS
GO THROUGH MANY HANDS,
BEFORE IT MEETS WITH A KNAVE THAT WILL STOP ITS PROGRESS.
THIS IS A TRICK OF MINE
FOR
DOING
A DEAL OF GOOD WITH A LITTLE MONEY.
I AM NOT RICH ENOUGH TO AFFORD MUCH IN GOOD WORKS,
AND SO AM OBLIGED TO BE CUNNING AND MAKE THE MOST OF A LITTLE.
WITH BEST WISHES FOR THE SUCCESS OF YOUR MEMORIAL,
AND YOUR FUTURE PROSPERITY.
I AM, DEAR SIR,
YOUR MOST OBEDIENT SERVANT,
BENJAMIN FRANKLIN

Staios Goat Cheese

This is a packaging for Staios Goat Cheese, a brand whose name comes from Greek god of shepherds and cheese-making, Aristaios. The brand aims to deliver the finest cheese in the U.S.

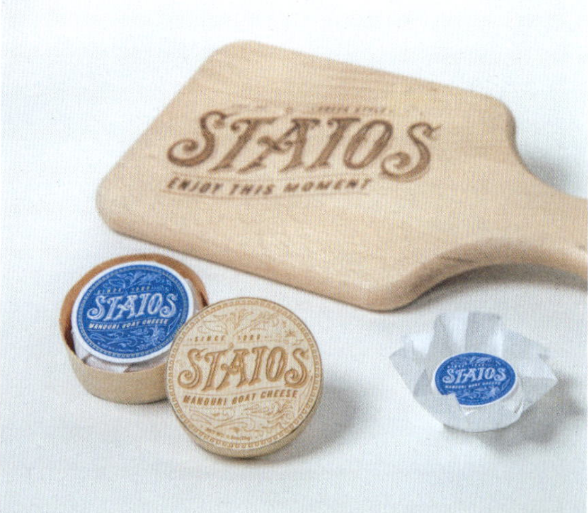

designer:

Jialu (Cece) Li

GREEK STYLE
SINCE 1989
STAIOS
MANOURI GOAT CHEESE
NET WT 40oz(1.1kg)

Believe Playing Cards

Believe playing cards is a uniquely crafted deck inspired by the Wayang Kulit (Shadow Puppets) of the Island of Java, Indonesia. It has meticulously replicated the details and intricacy of Wayang Kulit, incorporating mythical eastern elements with modern western design. The card back features a unique Wayang Shadow Puppet with a beautiful lotus flower while the card faces display custom-made pips, indices and courts. Each Ace also has its unique design and pattern.

studio:
System6Magic

designer:
Ipung kurniawan

QUALITY PLAYING CARDS ~ THE U.S PLAYING CARD COMPANY
PLAYING
CARDS
MADE IN
THE U.S.A
QUALITY PLAYING CARDS ~ THE U.S PLAYING CARD COMPANY

J
J

Q
Q

K
K

Maddhu

Maddhu, a name with origin in Hindi Bengali idiom meaning "sweet", is a family business based in Guadalajara, Mexico, which specializes in the production and marketing of desserts and confectionery, especially maccaroons. The designers took inspiration from the Islamic and Hindu Mudejar aesthetics of the 19th century, when India was witnessing British colonialism and a golden time in trade and packaging design. The central character of Maddhu is an elephant, an animal representative of India that evokes tenderness, sweetness and elegance.

studio:

MONOTYPO Studio

designer:

Daniel Barba López

ESTD. MADDHU 2012
Postres y algo más
CONFITERÍA & POSTRERÍA
FACEBOOK / INSTAGRAM: MADDHU.MX
contacto@maddhu.Com | MADDHU.COM
3317302158
ESTD. MADDHU 2012
CONFITERÍA & POSTRERÍA
MADDHU.COM

Gauri

Since the brand name Gauri was derived from the Goddess who has a gold body, designers decided that it should tell a story about a collection of golden tastes of Indian sweets. Based on the idea that every sweet is like a piece of gold, they identified the brand with unique luxury patterns, with a combination of a gold and black colors.

studio:

SAMOSOBOY

designer:

Danil Zdorov

art director:

Alexander Sydorenko

MENU
Ampita
Anyor
Raj
Govardhan
Balaram
Vrinda
Hari
Holi
Ananda
Gopal
Radharani
Rama
Gauranga
Jai
Burfi
Makhanchor
Haribol
Luglu
Shakti
Balaram

GAURI
GAURI

Albatros

This maritime-themed branding was created for a residential compound with a great view of the city and river. Promoting general maritime concepts, the design aims to represent a comfortable and peaceful life by the sea. Two kinds of pattern for external and internal communications have been created to arrive at a unique identity that sets Albatros aside from its peers.

studio:

SUPERMARKET Branding Agency

Есть у котика призванье. Кот морской — вот это званье!
Славный синий кит
Он плывет по океану,
Удивляет всех фонтаном.
Море дремлет, в море штиль,
Тишина на сотни миль.
В океане
КИТ
живет,
Шириною с пароход.
Словно остров
он огромный.
А на ощупь
КИТ
— холодный!
Дядя Кит - он самый-самый:
Самый важный, самый главный,
Самый добрый и большой,
и, как небо - голубой
Море дремлет,
в море
штиль,
Тишина на сотни миль.
Море ласково и мило,
Успокоилось,
застыло.
На волнах качаясь
Капитан, капитан, улыбнитесь
Ведь улыбка — это флаг корабля,
Капитан, капитан, подтянитесь
Только смелым покоряются моря
Крепко-крепко сжали створки
Маленькие устрицы.
Эй, ракушки-черноморки!
Доброе вам утрецо!
Мы, звёзды, как феи невиданных снов,
Раскрашены в сотни
светлей и спокойней
от наших лучей.
Высоко взмыл альбатрос,
Спрятал в облако
свой нос.
В облаке не видно
носа
Белой птицы альбатроса.
Как-то юнга
Дудочкин
Бросил в море лот,
И на эту
удочку
Клюнул кашалот
В море,
в зарослях
игривых,
Вьется пламя огонька —
Раздувают
воды гриву
Норовистого
конька
Он морской
хамелеон
Да ещё
в полоску,
Среди водорослей он,
Незаметный
просто.
Мачты пахнут облаками,
Флаги - синими ветрами
Друг за другом мчится стая,
Волны телом разрезая,
То хвосты, то снова спины,
Все вперёд плывут дельфины.
Любит море,
небо, ветер
Тот летающий матрос!
Крылья всех длинней на свете,
И зовется
— альбатрос!
Тепло, как хочется на море
На пляж, где плещутся прибои
Где нет забот, проблем, хлопот
Лишь море, солнце и песок
Забыть про все дела на свете,
Пахнет камбуз корабля.
Глубиною — якоря.
Штормом, солнцем, океаном
Теплоход пропах туманом.
Солью — палубные доски,
Качаясь спит очень сладко
У соседки Барсик кот, он на форточке живёт
У сибирского кота не житьё, а красота.
Толстый краб ползет, спешит,

Otoño 100% Ibérico De Huelva

Otoño is 100% Ibérico Spanish ham made from free-range pigs raised in a sustainable environment. The respect for tradition and a dedication to safeguarding the environment is crucial to the brand's essence. The packaging collection functions as a set, where each of the three main products is represented by its own tree species. The leaf blueprints provide each product with individual identity, thereby enriching the brand experience of the whole product range and creating a strong link to the brand name "Otono" (Autumn).

studio & designer:

Tres Tipos Gráficos

OTOÑO
OTOÑO
OTOÑO
En Otoño conservamos la tradición y los valores del producto 100% Ibérico. Nuestros cerdos crecen en libertad en la dehesa de Huelva, donde se alimentan de forma natural, con la mejor bellota de nuestra tierra.
In Otoño we preserve the tradition and values of the 100% *Ibérico* products. We breed our free range pigs in the Mediterranean *dehesa*, where they enjoy a natural and exclusive acorn based diet.

OTOÑO
OTOÑO
OTOÑO

OTOÑO
Paleta de bellota
100% Ibérica

OTOÑO
Lomo de bellota
100% Ibérico

Gao-Muoi:

Rice and Salt

The first product of GM Creative is "Gao-Muoi", a plain and traditional expression meaning "rice and salt" in Vietnamese language. The project represents the studio's desire to bring their hearts and souls to their designs as well as to make ends meet.

studio:
GM Creative Studio

designer:
GM Creative

Self-Promotion

This self-promotion project aims to invite curiosity and interaction with the inspiration from the Russian Matrjoschka dolls. The application consists of a packaging that has to be opened and folded up in different ways in order to get to the final object that reveals a QR-code leading to the designer's website. By looking closer, the "stars" reminding reviewers of the universe reveal themselves as the dielines of the packaging structure.

designer:

Alessia Sistori

CRAFTS
packaging
paper sculpture
bookbinding
printing techniques
experimental design
ILLUSTRATOR
PHOTOSHOP
INDESIGN
LIGHTROOM
PREMIERE
AFTEREFFECTS
GLYPHS
A1

Russian Bear Urban Expressions

This is a winning artwork by Hylton Warburton for the design competition "Urban Expressions" held by Russian Bear Vodka. The bottles were then produced as a limited edition for selected clients and consumers.

studio:
StudioWarburton

designer:
Hylton Warburton

RUSSIAN BEAR
DRUM
HOTEL
HIGH LIFE
PREMIUM
RUSSIAN BEAR
VODKA

Mmnmall Black Box Mockup

This mockup featuring an elegant and exclusive packaging was prepared on the basis of pictures taken in a professional studio. The visual identification was designed to illustrate the possibilities of editing a mockup.

studio:
MÏCU™ Studio

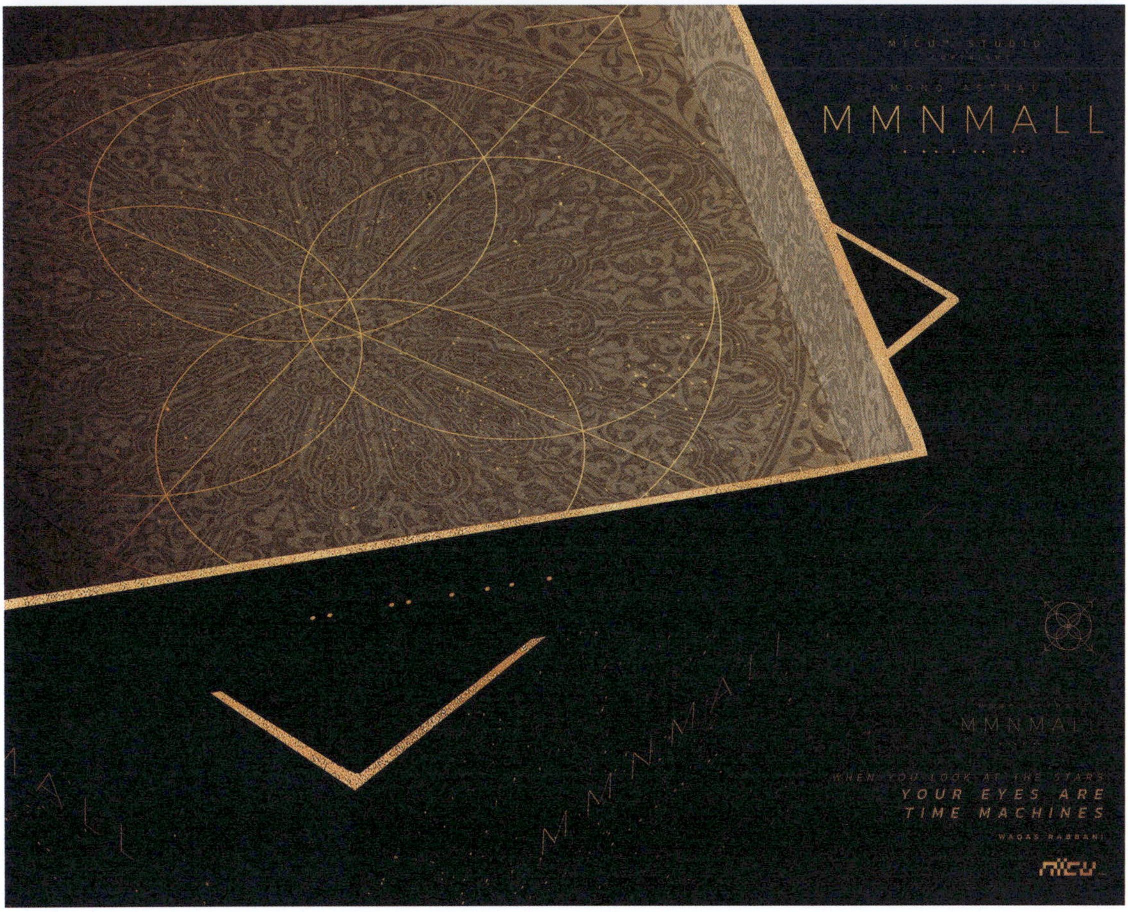

MICU STUDIO

MONO ASTRAL

MMNMALL

MMNMALL

WHEN YOU LOOK AT THE STARS
YOUR EYES ARE
TIME MACHINES

WAQAS RABBANI

micu

Aguafuerte

El Aguafuerte is a distinctive canteen. The studio sought to represent the essence of the rural Mexican drunk, one who is drowning in the agua fuerte bottle. In consideration of the historical and cultural importance of this place in the city, the designers rescued all the graphic elements of the old days and dipped into original resources to achieve a fully Chihuahuan identity.

designer:
Estudio Yeyé

EL AGUAFUERTE CANTINA BRAVA. 100%
CHIHUAHUENSE
VICTORIA
NO
823
CENTRO
DESDE
2013

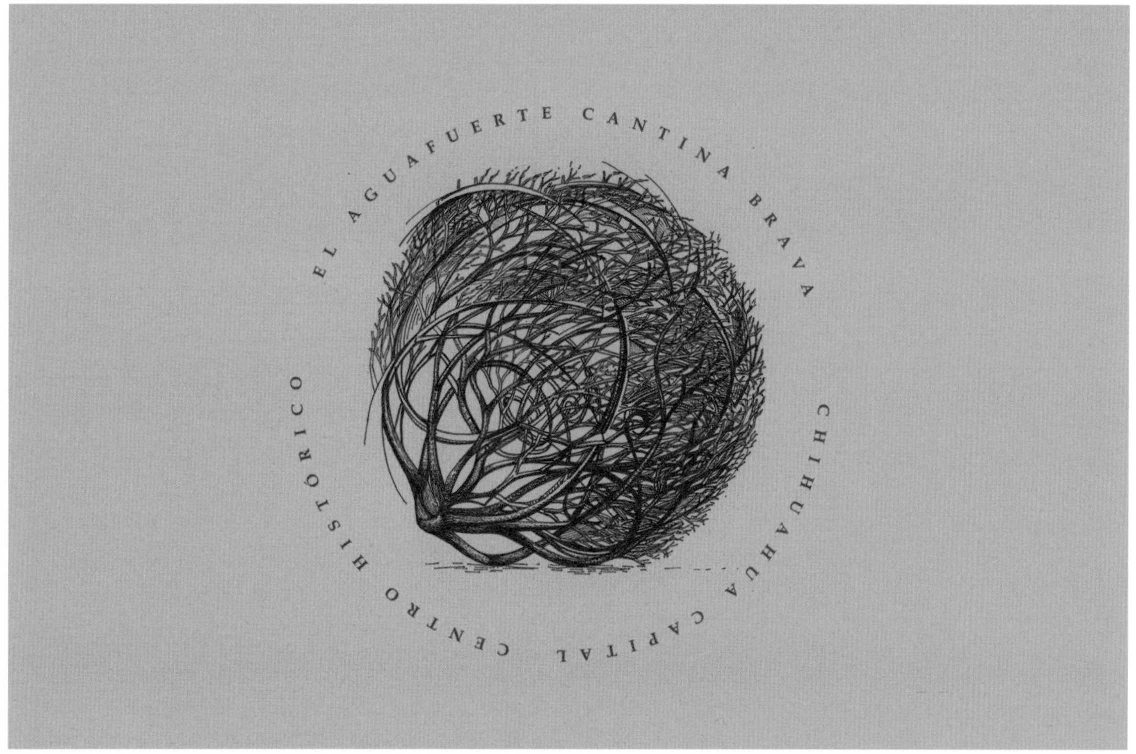
EL AGUAFUERTE CANTINA BRAVA
CHIHUAHUA CAPITAL
CENTRO HISTORICO

Rescate tipográfico y gráfico a partir de las placas publiciarias originales, impresión en técnica tradicional de la época

Paris Croissant

The new identity and packaging for the premium brand Paris Croissant, part of the SPC Korean Group, is based on the French"art de vivre". 2S Global Design's team brought a premium French touch to each communication medium of Paris Croissant.

Because Paris is the French capital of bakery, 2S drew its inspiration from ancient bakery styles. The typography is refned through traditional and modern perspectives. The wheat symbol was included to reinforce the brand's universe, while different versions of the logo were created for each communication medium.

studio:
2S Global Design

designer:
Sophie Schott, Florence Bezies

QUALITÉ ARTISANALE - VIENNOISERIE - BOULANGERIE - PÂTISSERIE - SALON DE THÉ - CHOCOLATIER -
PARIS
CROISSANT

PARIS
CROISSANT

PARIS CROISSANT

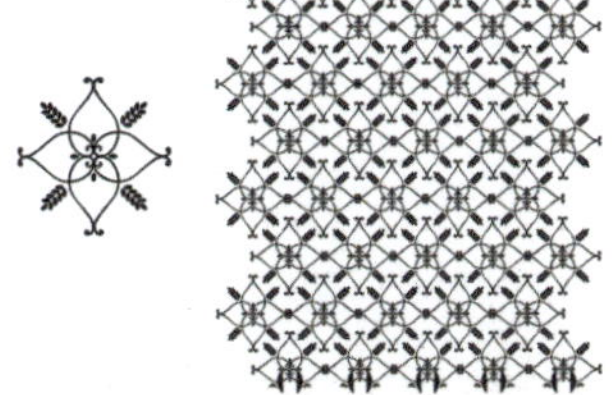

PARIS
CROISSANT
COFFRET CADEAUX
PARIS
CROISSANT
COFFRET CADEAUX

PARIS
CROISSANT

Heston's Fantastical Feasts

The designer has worked with Grade Design and Bloomsbury publishing to create illustrations and typography design for Heston Blumenthal's Cook book *Heston's Fantastical Feasts*.

studio:
Ginger Monkey

designer:
Tom Lane

Pathfinder Design Award

Pathfinder Design Award was a project to satirize and criticize the reckless design contests that were held just to get creative ideas and designs in a cheap price. Participants get only certification and little money. To show this, the designer created a design award and initiated an event. Its identity fully adopted the most authoritative graphic style, "Ornament", to show illusory authority of these contests. As a result, a lot of designs from different countries were submitted and all of them were awarded.

designer:

Won-kyoung Seo

DESIGN AWARD
PATHFINDER
2014
Certification
Award
PATHFINDER
POSTER
GRAND PRIX
CONGRATURATIONS TO
LEE, JUNGHUI
THE PATHFINDER DESIGN AWARD
WE GATHERED TOGETHER
TO SEEK MORE EFFECTIVE COMMUNICATION METHODS,
AND PRAISE AND ENCOUGAHE THEM TO PROTECT
BASIC IDEA OF DESIGN AWARD.
The Foreman of International Jury
SEO, WON-KYOUNG
JUNE, 2014
CA

DESIGN AWARD
PATHFINDER
2014
2014
Pathfinder

Design Award
모든 이들을 위한 디자인 어워드
Pathfinder Design Award 2014™ 개최
응모자격 제한없음 접수기간 2014.05.12(월) ~ 06.12(목)
응모분야
포스터 부문 디자인 포스터, 레터링, 인포그래픽 및 단일 스프레드 결과물
타이포그래피 부문 북디자인, 책자, 브로셔 등 복수 스프레드 결과물 (북커버 응모 가능)
브랜딩 부문 CI, BI, 사인시스템을 포함한 모든 브랜드 아이덴티티 디자인 결과물
UI/UX 부문 모바일 어플리케이션 디자인을 포함한 모든 종류의 인터랙티브 결과물
모션그래픽 부문 단편, 초단편영화, 2D 및 3D 모션그래픽, VFX 및 모든 영상 결과물
일러스트레이션 부문 일러스트레이션, 혹은 일러스트가 포함된 모든 종류의 디자인 결과물
접수방법 웹하드에 이미지 형식(jpg, jpeg,150dpi / 영상은 75mb이하 mp4, mpg, mpeg)으로 업로드
홈페이지 참조 / pathfinderaward.org
주최 패스파인더 디자인 어워드 사무국
후원
CA
ORDINARY PEOPLE

Gawatt Coffee Shop

For a distinctive take-out coffee shop in steampunk style, the designers created different sizes of cups depending on the power charge of their "watt" contained—kilowatt, megawatt, and terawatt, since the brand name is reminiscent of the universal steam engine inventor or unit of power, delivering a joyful and exciting atmosphere to audience.

studio:
Backbone Branding

designer:
Karen Gevorgyan

art director:
Stepan Azaryan

illustrator:
Armenak Grigoryan

Urban Folklor

This poster was created for the Urban Folklor competition. The designer found it worthwhile to interpret the treasures of Hungarian folk art with the use of contemporary technique and style. The poster contains mostly floral ornaments. Some most occurring patterns were redesigned to supplement the original design.

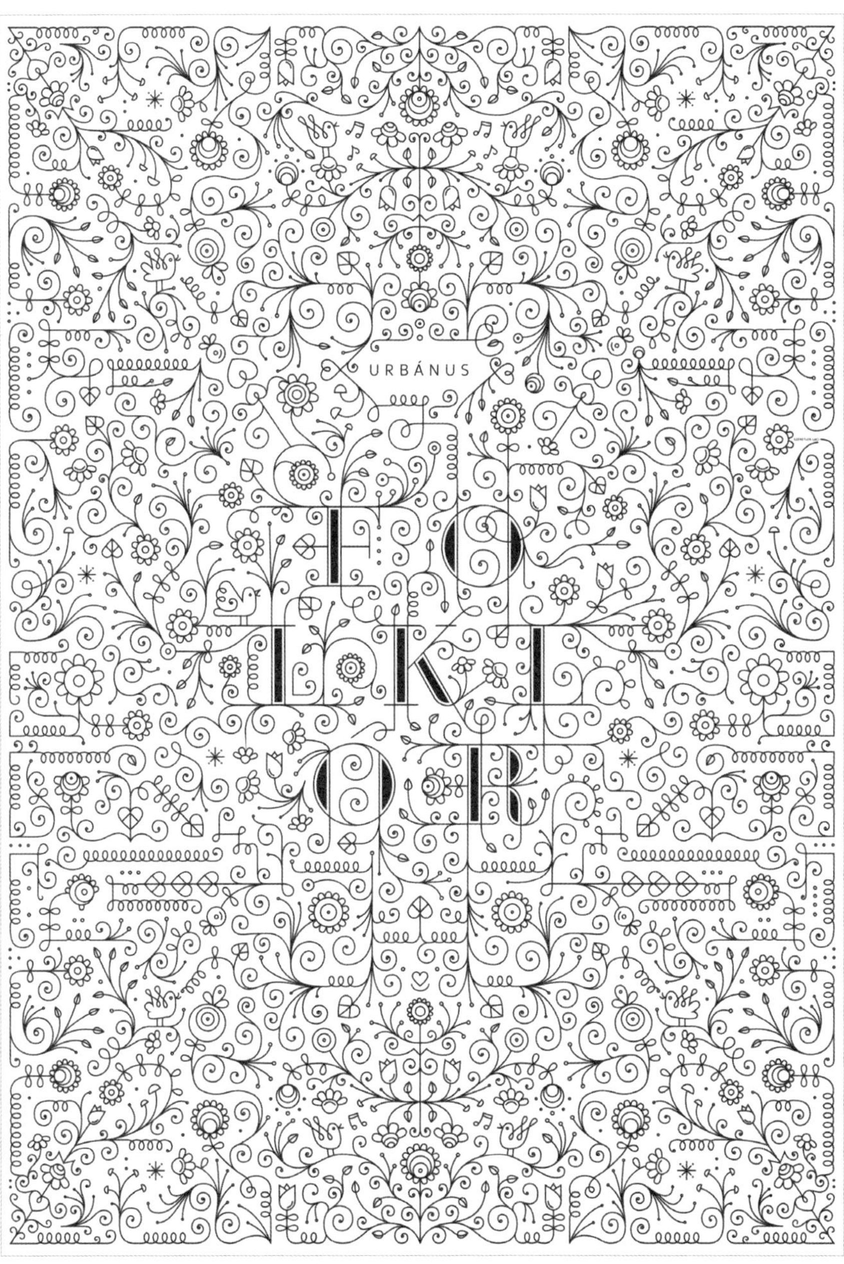

designer:

Boglárka Nádi

Cannes Data Portrait

Graphic designer and illustrator Yoaz has been invited and teamed up with other 10 artists for the challenge of creating "data portraits" of industry leaders and influencers who best represent the mix of creativity and data, while incorporating data gathered from public sources for the 2017 Cannes Lions. This work shows Yoaz's interpretation of Timothy Armoo with inspiration from street art, pop art and cubism.

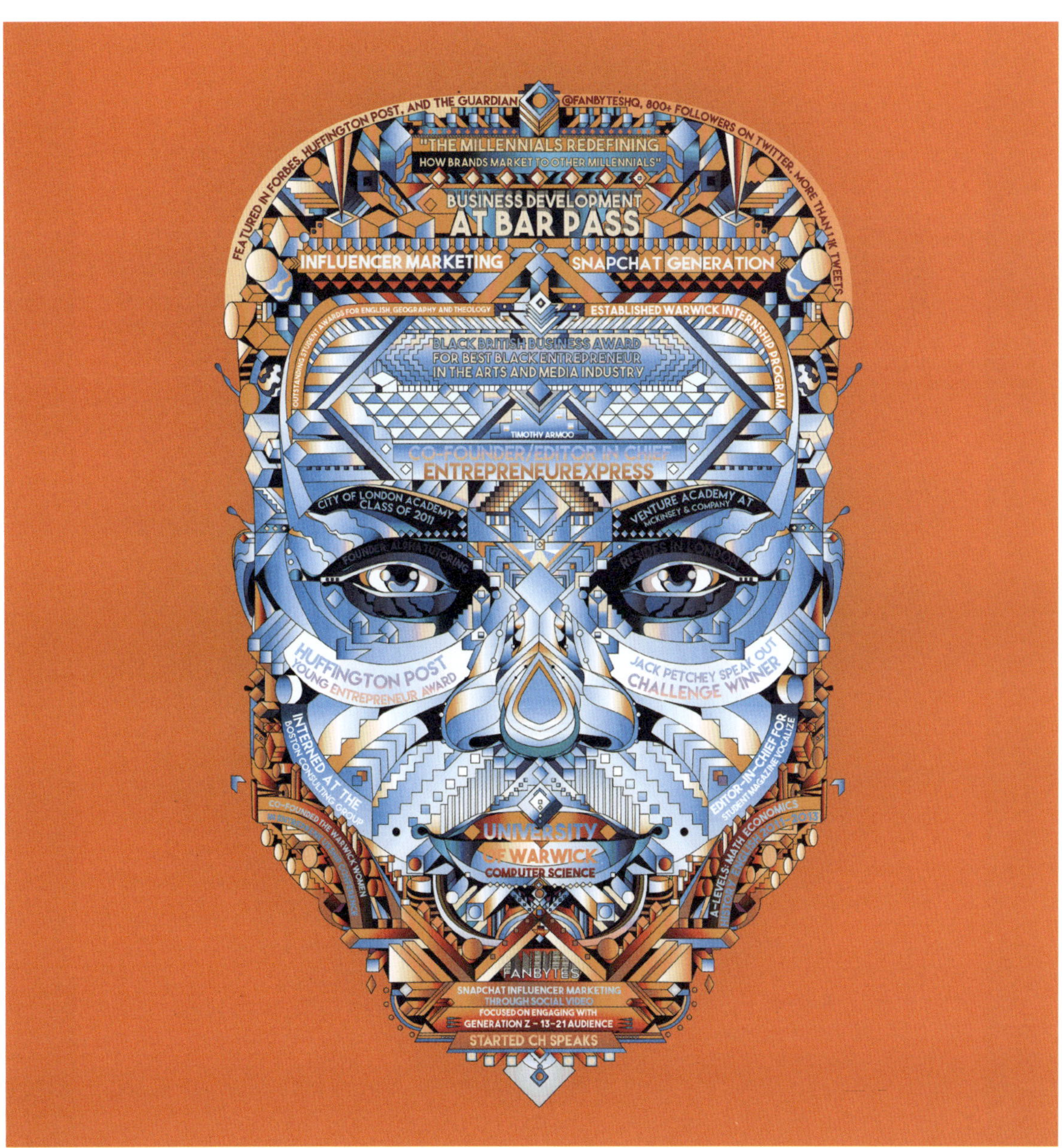

studio:

Adobe,

Wunderman

designer:

YoAz

Mekkanika Typeface

MEKKANIKA is a type-treatment-face inspired by the steampunk visual world. The mechanical look-like typeface was created by mixing and merging technical drawing of composition pieces of classic mechanics. The sharpness of the detail stays intact even when scaling.

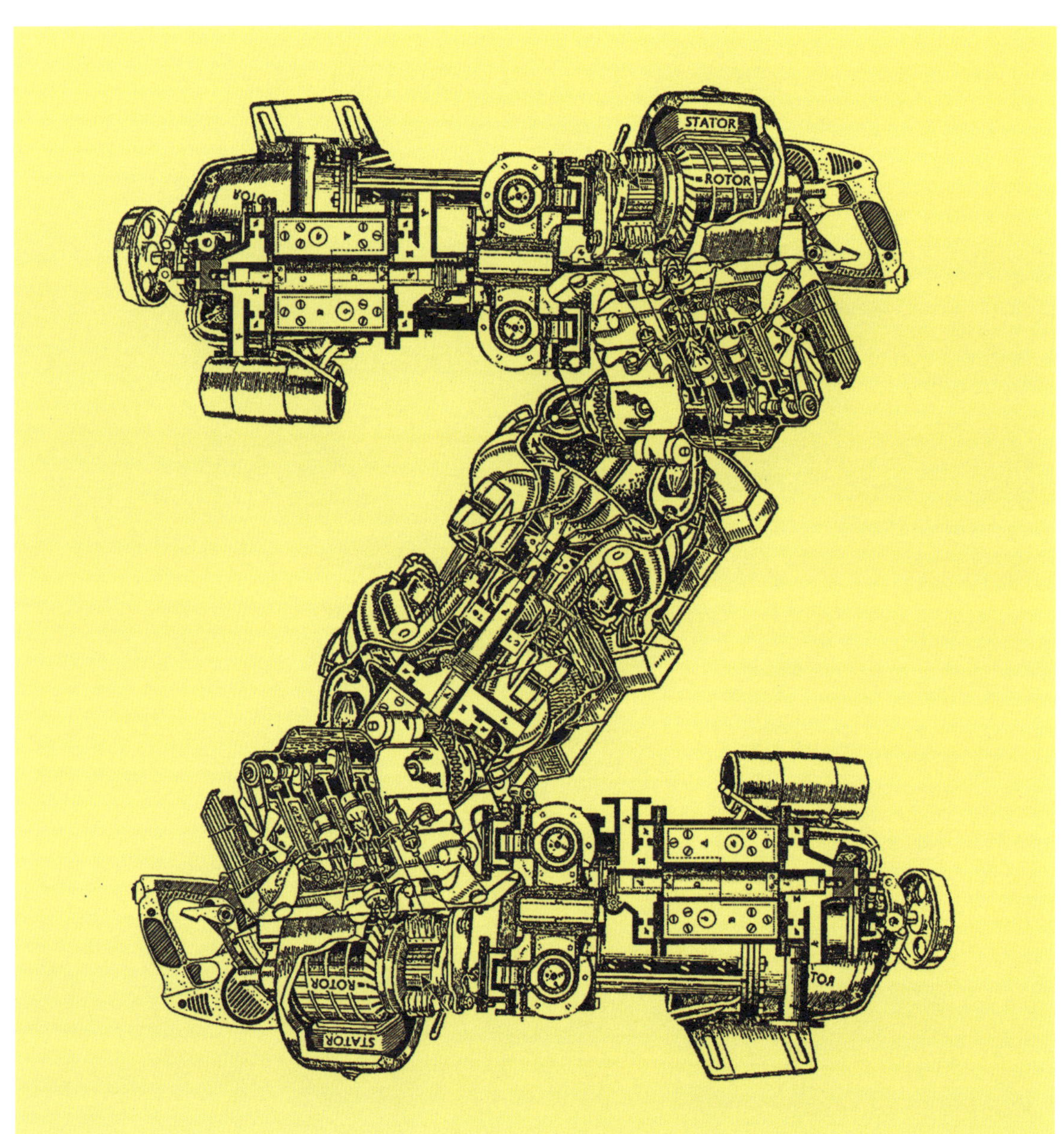

designer:

Riccardo Sabatini

MEK
KAN
IKA

The Happy 8

The Happy 8 is a high-quality chain hotel brand of Malaysia. The brand is enlightened from the combination of Nanyang culture and art. The design was inspired by the vibrant colors in the local system, mysterious national symbols as well as the inclusive multicultural. The Brand identity system reinterprets the unique culture and has achieved a strong coherent brand experience while giving uniqueness to every touch-points. The designers envision to lead a cultural and artistic journey for the customers through the design.

studio:

1983ASIA

designer:

SUSU & YAO

戲童圖

TheHappy
Eight

TheHappy
Eight

The Happy
Eight

The Happy
Eight

MAVEM

The branding and packing for a Portuguese aguardente are based on the idea of discovery—the key to the Golden Age of Portugal in the 15th century. To express and house the Mavem brand concept and story, the designers adopted the Azulejos art with its distinctive blue and white color identity. The rich promise of the brand is expressed in a Manuelino style, inspired by the maritime and mythological world of discoveries. The Mavem brand creation journey shows that authority and roots are not reserved to old brands.

studio:
MEGUSTA

designer:

Laurent Bouclier, Henri Sizaret, Pierre Courbon

index

ACKNOWLEDGEMENTS

We would like to thank all the designers and contributors who have been involved in the production of this book. Their contributions have been indispensable in its compilation. We would also like to express our gratitude to all the producers for their invaluable opinions and assistance throughout this project. And to the many others whose names are not credited but have made specific input in this book, we thank you for your continuous support.

FUTURE COOPERATIONS

If you wish to participate in SendPoints' future projects and publications, please send your website or portfolio to

editor01@sendpoints.cn